Robert Bussey has been practicing Law in Louisiana for the past 35 years or so. He lived his formative years in a suburb of Chicago. He then moved to Texas, which he considers his adoptive state, and lived for some 10 years in Austin. While in Texas, he started to pedal thousands of miles around the country on his bicycle. Those journeys took him through much of the Midwest and the western part of the United States. He then married and moved to Louisiana and was immersed in the Cajun culture through his in-laws who resided in the small town of Ville Platte. Louisiana continues to be a boiling pot of many cultures.

There are so many people to whom I owe a debt of gratitude. I would be remiss not to mention the following: Mom, Dad, my four sisters, my childhood friends, my wife (Phyllis), my kids (Sara, Colin, and Martine), my grandchildren (Peyton, Caroline, Audrey Ann, Parker, and Jamey). Those family members have inspired me and put up with me through thick and thin. I have two special people who have read my poems and commented on them: Maria and Marilyn. I cannot begin to express how much I have appreciated their help, understanding, and encouragement. To my friends: Clark, Stacey, Steve, and Lindsey—you are the best money cannot buy.

Robert Bussey

WALK WITH ME

Some Time, Some Where, Some How

AUSTIN MACAULEY PUBLISHERS™

LONDON • CAMBRIDGE • NEW YORK • SHARJAH

Ordering Information
Quantity sales: Special discounts are available on quantity purchases by corporations, associations, and others. For details, contact the publisher at the address below.

Publisher's Cataloging-in-Publication data
Bussey, Robert
Walk with Me

ISBN 9781638296577 (Paperback)
ISBN 9781638296560 (Hardback)
ISBN 9781638296584 (ePub e-book)

Library of Congress Control Number: 2023908668

www.austinmacauley.com/us

First Published 2023
Austin Macauley Publishers LLC
40 Wall Street, 33rd Floor, Suite 3302
New York, NY 10005
USA

mail-usa@austinmacauley.com
+1 (646) 5125767

There is a person who has read every poem I have written, Maria O. She has done so without asking for anything in return. She has encouraged me to continue setting down my ideas, thoughts, emotions, observations in poetic form. While she lives hundreds of miles away from me, has her family to look after, she has always found time to comment on what I have sent. Poetry tends to be a solitary endeavor. It is special when you find someone who will share in your journey. My wife, Phyllis, has given me the space, time, and understanding to write. Audrey Ann, my granddaughter, taught me to again look through the eyes of a child. Those three, Audrey Ann, Phyllis and Maria O, have made this book possible in so many ways. My hat is off to them!

Table of Contents

Of Children

Walk with Me

Walk with me, said the black child.
Feel the warmth of my hand.
Feel the strength of my muscles.
Feel the blood flowing in my veins.
See my smile.
Hear my laugh.

Walk with me, said the brown child.
Feel the warmth of my hand.
Feel the strength of my muscles.
Feel the blood flowing in my veins.
See my smile.
Hear my laugh.

Walk with me, said the red child.
Feel the warmth of my hand.
Feel the strength of my muscles.
Feel the blood flowing in my veins.
See my smile.
Hear my laugh.

Walk with me, said the yellow child.
Feel the warmth of my hand.
Feel the strength of my muscles.
Feel the blood flowing in my veins.
See my smile.
Hear my laugh.

Walk with me, said the white child.
Feel the warmth of my hand.
Feel the strength of my muscles.
Feel the blood flowing in my veins.
See my smile.
Hear my laugh.

Walk with us.
They all said.
See us run and jump.
Listen to us laugh and chatter.
Feel the glow in our hearts.

We don't like hunger.
We don't like pain.
Hate needs to find some other place to play.
Hearing friends cry an emotional drain.
Please don't lead us astray.

We want to be happy.
We want to be free.
We want a chance to grow like little trees.
We want to sing and smile.
Walk with us for an hour, or a day, or for just a mile while being bold.
Walk with us, not beside us, but with us.
Give us your love and we will return it tenfold.

WALK with Me #2
(Mother and Son)

Walk with me, said the mother to her son.
Hold my hand tight.
Don't let go.
I want to show you some wonderful sights.
Just around the block or so.

The sun will warm us on this gentle spring day.
Birds are making their nests.
You will see them work and play.
Squirrels will be our guests.
Butterflies and bees light the way.

The animals and insects are so busy.
Learn from them that work is good.
The rewards are many.
The warm, dry, nest.
So much like a house.
Watch the ants work as a team.
Carrying food for their ant hill.
Teamwork helps builds many a dream.
Teamwork and a strong will.
As you grow you will have many goals to fulfill.

But we also have to be careful.
Because ants can bite and sting.
Not everything is soft and beautiful.
Sometimes you must watch for a hurtful thing.

But not today as we make our way.
Along our journey, and along yours too.
We will meet many people.
Each of them different.
Each unique.
Try to treat them all with inquisitive interest.

Like old Mr. James.
See him peeking out his door.
All gray, wrinkly, and stooped over.
He was once the police chief.
Lots of tales about worldly matters.
Listen closely if he speaks.

While you still play with your friends
Spend some time with your elders
If you can.
They have been down many paths.
They have many stories to tell.

Look up in the sky.
Do you see those clouds?
Can you feel the warm sun?
Smell the air.
Every plant and creature needs them.

It is hard to imagine,
But all things are connected
In some form or fashion.
The birds, the squirrels, and you and I, all need the sun.
We all need the watery rain.
We all need fresh air to breathe.

Are you still holding tight?
We are almost home.
I can see our porch light.

Look there's your favorite garden gnome.
Your eyes are sparkling so bright.

Brother and sister are waiting for you.
Your first true friends.
The three of you are quite the sibling's stew.
Later, they can help you with your girlfriends.
Until then have fun, don't be blue.
Go ahead, run!

Walk with Me #4

Walk with me.
Said Sabah, a child from northern Iraq.
I am Yazidi.
I am told we are few.
Our religion a mixture of many.
Ancient Iranian religions, Judaism, Nestorian, Christianity and Islam.
Perhaps it should be called the world religion.
I am too young to give it a good definition.

My home was invaded and torn apart.
For years I hid from those with no heart.
I could not go to school.
I could not swim in any river or pool.
I stayed inside most every day.
I dared not venture out to play.
For five years I was in fear.
But now I know evil is not near.

Walk with me now.
Help me build my future.
Watch me walk to school with my book sack.
Past gutted buildings.
Along streets with memories so black.
Past the fields of many killings.
Walk towards my future with me.
My school will help set me free.

My mother likes to walk with me.
My friends are with me, too.
My teachers water my mental tree.
My studies my living glue.
Knowledge cannot be taken from me.
It sails upon the spoken word—a butterfly or bee.

Nazdar, my mother, wants the best for me.
She wants me to learn and grow.
With knowledge I shall learn to glow.
Perhaps someday I shall be a doctor.
Able to help others, right and proper.

Walk with me every day.
Tell me peace is here to stay.
That evil will not take you away.
Walk with me as I pray.
Walk with me, day after day after day.

Young Girl

She had the ability to make the sky smile when it was raining.
The gray clouds became beacons of light.
All the while she was gaining and gaining
Knowledge that made her glow ever so bright.

Her hair shone with utter joy.
Filling the world around her with love and compassion.
Dangling its laughter as if a ploy.
Waiting for a reaction.

Beams of light surrounded her and those around her.
Warmth was how she greeted you and everyone.
Norms did not distract her or contain her.
She had no guard to let down.

Rainbows colored her eyes.
The scent of fall, summer and spring clung to her, longing to survive.
She saw with the pureness of a butterfly.
Sending words of love with her every movement and smile.
She danced with every step,
Lightly touching the ground,
A smile of innocence not contained.
Darting about with joy unbound,
Listening intently for a special sound.

Reaching the door with determined intent.
Opening it as if it were her heart.
Having heard the steps arrive.
Letting in someone she knew quite well.

Satisfied.

Advice to the Young

Young one recently born exploring life
Unknown by you that I often see myself
In your eyes so pure with joy close inside.
Enjoying each moment pure by itself.
As you grow, watch closely those around you.
For they will touch your warmest living soul.
Stay within what you know to be well true.
Someday you will find another and breakthrough.
Perhaps someone spiritually true.
With fatherly concern I shall watch you.
Often from a distance but at heart so close.
Your happiness my utmost open concern.
In time you will realize your birthright
Remember to stand tall and ever upright.

New Life

My life changed the day you arrived on earth.
For in my aged years you made me young.
A child creating a child of old clay.
A baby making an elder feel new.
The wonder in your eyes craving warm hands.
Your cry bringing joy to so many listening.
New life bringing life, joy, to those around.
Hunger anew crying in the still night.
How you changed the world around everyone.
From the moment you arrived from heaven.
Being cradled gently in arms so strong.
Seeing the world awake before your eyes.
Letting others experience new life.
Magically transforming my old breath.

Childhood Days

As gold as the rays of the sun.
Shimmering and waving with life.
Making everyone realize that life is often on the run.
Waiting for someone to see what is really so easy to see.
Hair as light and flowing as the day is long.
Waiving with pure fun.

The sun has never be so bright.
Nor could it be so warm.
Dancing in circles ever so tight.
Skipping along an unexplained path.
Smelling and tasting the scent of flowers in the wind.

Joy for joy's sake.
Smiling for no reason at all.
Laughing with nothing at stake.
Squirming with delight and standing tall.
Not afraid to fall.

The innocence of childhood.
Finding fun, being totally alive.
Always finding something good.
A regular energy beehive.
Shifting into pleasure overdrive

Ah, to play outside on a summer day.
With your friends, old and new.
Running, skipping, laughing all the way.

Playing with words—moo, boo, dew, roux.
Nothing to make you blue.

Magical, golden, childhood days.
Moments, memories, etched in time.
Looking back, remembering the fun ways.
So many remembrance shrines.
Kick the can one more time!

The Kids Ballgame

Who ran into When one day.

Smiling, they skipped over to Why's house.

Can Why come out to play they would both say.

What was already at Why's house.

So, Who, When, Why and What decided to play.

Running to the park, they bumped into Where.

She was not happy that day.

Your had pushed her down and Where had a nasty bruise on her knee.

Who, When, Why and What invited Where to the park.

The five of them started to run.

But Your got in their way.

"Your, get out of our way," Who, What, Why, When and Where did say.

Your replied, "I also want to play."

That was okay, since they needed more to have fun that day.

Then How came from around the corner.

"Can I also play?" asked How.

"Sure," said Who, What, Why, Where and Your.

So now they had seven.

Almost enough.

But they needed a few more.

"It takes nine to play this game," exclaimed Who.

At least two more needed.

Their and I were already at the park.

That made nine.

"Perfect," howled Who.

"Let the game begin," screamed What.

But then they realized they were only one team.

Another nine were needed for this game of baseball.

"My gosh," Who, What, When, Why, Where, Your, Their,

How and I all shouted.

"Just where shall we find another nine," they all wondered.

About that time, We and Me got off their bikes.

"Hey," they called out.

"Some friends will be arriving soon."

Down the street everyone could see the group.

Carrying mitts and baseball bats.

Marching to a song.

Along came Our, It, Us, This, Those, These, and Everybody.

Ah, another nine.

So the teams got in a line.

Who, What, When, Where, Why, Your, Their, How and I in one.

We, Me, Our, It, Us, This, Those, These and Everybody in the other.

Just one more needed, a home plate ump.

Someone older.

Someone with authority.

Someone with knowledge of the game.

Someone never to be questioned.

Someone quick with words.

Someone with fast feet.

Someone with keen eyes.

Sure nuff, Yogi Bear, came to the rescue.

"Play Ball!" Yogi exclaimed.

The teams played all afternoon.

Playing till almost dark.

Tied at 2 apiece.

What was last at bat.

A homer would do it.

The team was screaming as the ball left the bat.

The crack could be heard round the world.

What rounded the bases and jumped on home plate.

The team lifted What up in the air.

The game was done.

Who, What, Where, Why, Your, Their, How and I had won!

At the Beach

Laughter on the wind.
Joy saluting the sunshine.
Feet racing the tide.
Trying not to get wet.
Peace refined and redefined.
Laughter renewing God's design.
Forget sadness, it has nowhere to hide
Elation wins this summertime beach bet.

The chorus of laughing joy.
Permeates to the core.
Impossible to keep it out.
Come on…SHOUT!
Dance to the summer fun…deploy.
Join us on the sandy beach dance floor.
Shake it and work it out!
Yeah, now you know what it's all about!

Flowers in Hand

She appears with many flowers in both hands.
A gentle smile adorns her radiance.
The world shines in her bright eyes, viewing lands.
Sounds surrounded those that see her pure brilliance.
Young child, you have so many years left here.
Your smile, your radiance, touching many.
Keep your gentle, warm glow, without dire fear.
Your love for life, for others, share with plenty.
Keeping always your common, informed, sense.
Your knowledge will aide you through many times.
Let not others erect around you a fence.
A fence to diminish your warm free vines.
Constantly bring warmth, Light, Art, Love to all.
Within you such strength letting you stand tall.

New Life (2)

A new soul enters our earthly planet.
Innocent of any human faults or sins.
Feeling Love of adults all around him.
Brought into this world with Love and sure hands.
Surrounded by caring people much skilled.
With knowledge amassed over many years.
His needs addressed now…weeks, months, years.
As he grows, his needs becoming complex.
Those around him still there to provide…care.
Advice coming from many directions.
The young child growing in the sun.
Learning to recognize love, truth, hard work.
Innocence lasts only a few short years.
Treasure every moment, encourage love.

Growth

Each child must grow.
Thoughts mature we know.
Eventually leaving the nest.
Heart filled with love.
Searching for Life's best.

Young Child with a Future

Young child with so many years to roam this place.
Remember to keep an open, clear, mind.
So much instruction lies before your face.
Important to smile, laugh, and be so kind.
The world rejoices when you dance and sing.
Your education so important now.
The path of your life like a wavy, strong, string.
On your path you will meet people with Tao.
Knowledge they will impart for you to learn.
Teachers they are with much for you to gain.
Wisdom streams from their minds and mouths to you.
Carefully listen inquisitive child.
Be strong, be sure, be kind, be fun and mild.
This world beckons you to live many rich years.

Do Not Sit Alone

Young, gorgeous lady sitting so alone.
Looking left, right, then gravely straight ahead.
Your bench missing sweet, romantic, presence.
Cold, lonely, a shame to be without any.
The world a playground for young to romp, play.
Open your eyes so joy can be clear seen.
Live not in sadness, but in sublime joy.
Those around waiting, hoping for a chance.
Dance with all your might while you are still able.
Leave your sadness behind where it belongs.
Joy of love, unblemished friendship, rejoice.
Find comfort in the arms of another.
Waste not your time on this Holy grand earth.
Find a mate, procreate, enjoy your rich life.

Walk with Me #41

My name is Adriel.
I live in Albania.
My friends are Elira, Agon and Daniel.
Take a walk with me.

My country is small.
Much less people than New York City.
It borders the Adriatic Sea.
We have mountains that are very tall.

For many years we were under an iron fist.
A government that held us back.
Worrying you were on some blacklist.
Freedom put us on the right track.

Education, once denied, now the norm.
Literacy a crowning gem.
Schooling free after much reform.
For all of us, not just them.

Poverty still a thundering concern.
Many young friends forced to work.
The whole family to live must earn.
Perhaps panhandling or being a store clerk.

So happy poverty decreasing.
Friends happily releasing.
Freedom's increasing.
Jobs improving.

Child trafficking a major problem.
Friends instantly gone.
Not allowed to blossom.
Child pawn.

We have such natural beauty.
A shame that child abuse exists.
Amongst such wonders truly.
Hoping it does not persist.

My future is bright.
If only we keep doing what is right.
Problems we can solve.
With much needed resolve.

Walk with me.
Hold my hand.
See Albania from mountains to sea.
Watch us as we finally stand.

The Little Oak Table

A child's oak table and two chairs.
Purchased with loving care.
For the first child.
Made for a child able to sit straight and tall.

It did its job well.
The first had almost outgrown it.
When the second one came.
A boy, much tougher
But the little table survived.

Then number three, another girl.
The table and chairs starting to show some scars.
But still sturdy enough.
By now some 12 years old.

Those children all matured.
Then left home.
For lives of their own.
But the table and chairs remained.

Memories engraved in its grain.
A paint mark here and there.
From a project.
Tenderly, eagerly done.

Those children married.
They had children of their own.
The table could not wait!

And so it was.
A second generation to support.

The table smiled.
Inwardly it glowed.
So much love had sat in its chairs.
Every fiber of its wood sang.

Four more found food, painting, books.
While sitting on its thrones.
A fifth growing.
But not quite old or strong enough yet.

No worry.
The oaken table could wait.
It's chairs as sturdy as the first day
Waiting was something it excelled at.

In the meantime.
A little facelift (by now it was some 30 years old).
Some sanding and loving care,
Listening to sweet music as it waited for the next in line.

The little table knew.
It would be needed once again.
Creating memories for the young.
Creating Joy was, after all, what it was all about!

Of Humor

Walk with Me #34

Walk with me, I am Jean Jacques from Mamou.
A small town in Cajun land.
Louisiana's heart and soul.
I grew up by Grand Louis Bayou, just outside of town.
I used to chase chickens during Mardi Gras as they flew.
One or two in the gumbo pot was sure to strike up the band.
While mama and papa danced the Cajun two step, like they was warmin' up
the North pole.
Nobody dat day had any frown.

I walked a mile or two to school.
Where they had me learn English as a second language.
Guess they was too stupid to understand Cajun French.
We already know how to pass a good time.
We ain't nobody's fool.
Ya'll need to lighten up and get rid of da baggage.
Mon Amie, get off dat bench.
Ya sit too much on da backside tool.

We got Fred's bar in da middle of town.
It be open one day a week.
But then it got the best Cajun, foot stomping, music that can be found.
When I was 14, they let me since I could see over da bar.
Fred's is a real town crown.
One that the whole world seek.
Everybody there dance in the round.
Leave on the dance floor one or two scar.

On da bayou we got some mighty catfish.
And an alligator or two.
Both real good fried up just right.
Delicacies up north, I hear.
Sure a heck of a lot better than any goldfish.
The kind ya find in a fancy zoo.
We give 'em a good battering, then fry 'em up real tight.
They good real good with one or two beer.

Santa Claus we know as Papa Noel.
He look pretty much the same.
But down here we leave him some crawfish etouffee.
Dat why he really get fat.
All da chillin' anxious to hear his bell.
Nobody sick dat night, nobody be lame.
Nobody actin real huffy or puffy.
If de do, den de just get a rat.

We grow lots of rice.
We grow some corn, soybeans, and cotton too.
We got da best lookin' women in da world.
Nuf said bout dat.
We also know how to throw da dice.
And, ah, we got da best of the best roux.
Yeah, dis quite de dream world.
Come cut de rug with me and lose some fat.

Mamou, it famous and that be good.
We got pirogues, one or two fais-do-dos a year
Come visit and you can be my Cher.
Come on down if you ever get an envie for some good cookin'.
Try out a second childhood. (If only for a day).
Down here a good time is always near.
Get ready to get down so tie up your hair.
Not much you be overlookin'.
Jus' make sure you be better than no good.

Yeah, Cher, down by da bayou we know how to act.

On Sundays we go to church.

But come Monday we ready to cut da rug again!

Dacin' ain't no sin.

The rest of de week, we work and das a fact.

But we always ready for some fun research.

Walk wit' me and talk wit' me before I get a mighty migraine.

Come sit wit' me by da bayou, so we can get away from all my crazy kin.

I be Jean Jacques, your best friend.

Sometime, Some of the Time, Some Time

Some of the time I sometimes question myself.
Sometimes I am darn certain, but not all the time.
Sometimes I wish she would give me a call sometime.
Questions are usually good most of the time.
Some of the time I feel like I have been placed upon a shelf.
Wondering if she will ever sometime come to see me.
Hoping that some of the time it will be worth the climb.
Praying for bliss in this time, and while still in my prime.

Can one expect bliss all the time?
Or should we be happy to experience it some time?
What in time can bring that bliss?
An occasional kiss, smile or hug, sometimes.
A few words set in a line.
A smile taking you out of the daily grime.
Something that you cannot miss.
Whether or not you are aware all the time or just some time.

It is hard to sometimes be true most of the time or even just some of the time.
Making your word your bond all of the time.
Keeping your word can be so dang hard.
Staying true to yourself even harder.
Try as you might you sometimes go astray.
Not easy to always walk that line.

So much easier not to go that extra yard.

Wishing that at least you could sometimes have sufficient ardor.

Such is the fate of living in a sometimes world.

Wondering if some time you might meet someone true.

Hoping that some of the time your instinct might be right.

Not all the time but just sometime.

Friends

One and Won were twins not identical.
But fraternal from a different umbilical.
They had some neighborhood friends.
To, Too, and Two, who loved deep knee bends.

The five of them were acquainted with Three.
Who lived across the street under the oak tree.
Near Three lived For, Four and Fore.
They could upset everyone else, making them real sore.

All of them were well acquainted with Almost Done, Totally Done and Over
Done.
Those brothers were always on the run.
There were three more that made this a hit.
Holy Shit, Totally Shit and their sister, Any Shit.

Oh, these friends could have lots of fun.
It was said they could never be outdone.
The hit of every party.
Their friendships, warm, full, and hearty.

Any Shit was usually outnumbered.
Especially when Totally Done and Holy Shit got together.
But she was tough as shit and did not care.
She was good at any dare.

The gang was invited to a party.
One, Won For, Fore and Four were a bit tardy.
Three, Two, To and Too were ahead of time.
They didn't want to stand in line.

Almost Done forgot his present.
Totally Done was just happy to go, so he went.
The cake was the best, it wasn't overdone,
commented Over Done.
As he beat Won, Too, and Holy Shit just for fun.

The brawl got out of hand.
Holy Shit, Totally Shit, For, Fore, and Four jumped right in.
They weren't going to take any shit from anyone.
Any Shit just sat and watched.
She didn't want to get her new dress splotched.
Almost Done appealed to everyone's senses.

"Stop this shit" he exclaimed.
Not knowing which Shit he meant created confusion.
So the rest just jumped on all the Shits...Totally,
Holy, and Any.
The brawl was almost done when Almost Done broke his leg.
When the rest emptied the keg.
When the hosts got down on their knees and begged
that the group would leave please, please, please!

Over Done and Totally Done knew when they weren't wanted.
Almost Done felt unwanted but was undaunted.
The Shits went to church, they gave a crap.
For, Fore and Four wanted to fight some more.
They wanted to win and even the score.
One, Won, To, Too and Two deided they were done.

This was no longer any fun.
Three was mellow about it all.
After all he did not have to take a fall.

He could not be blamed.
He had not been maimed.

There would be another day, another party.
Another chance for a friendship safari.
So, they bid each other adieu.
At least they had not run into What, When or Who.

Left, Left Over, Left Out

I was stumped.
Not sure anymore.
Right, rite, and write had become something more.
So I decided it was right to go left.
Left had to be the answer, right?

Left right or left of right.
Did it matter?
Could I deal with a left-over rite?
Right to be left…or perhaps wrong?
A left write could be in a song.
Or a left right in the key of C.

If I had a right to be left would I be lonely?
Or simply left of a right turn?
Left up, left down, left in, or left out.
Became perplexing.
Was I forgetting about some left rite?
Or did I simply have nothing left to write?

Sleeping on my left side was needed.
I am sure if left up to my left brain I would be alright.
Or was that my right to be right on my left?
My left brain would know if left alone!

Surely if left to write I would come up with the correct answer!
Help…I was not being left alone to figure out if I was right, or needed to write,
or was I creating a new rite.
I was left out in the cold!

What could be left to go wrong?
If I turned left for real.
Or if I turned left in my mind.
Did it really matter?
Was I missing out on anything that might be left?
So, I left my dilemma's party.
I left my dilemma's mind.
I walked intentionally out of town on the left side of the road.
Looking for the right view or a left over one.
I no longer cared.

I did not feel left out.
I did not ask to be left in.
Left up to me I would be left down!
If there was such a thing.
I kept walking left.
Finally, a fruit stand came into view.
On the left side of the road.
The right side was barren.
There I met Lefty who was selling leftover pies.
Ones from yesterday.
Half-eaten, with the Left side remaining.
He said it was the best he could do.
Since his wife had left him.
I left him leaning on the left side of the left wall of his fruit stand.
I continued my journey down the left lane.

Over a hill I came upon Left Alone stadium.
There was nothing around it.
No trees were left standing.
No streams or creeks left running.
No birds left nesting.
No dogs left barking.
The only entrance open was the one on the left side of this circular stadium.
I walked in.
Inside a team was practicing.

Geaux Left, Geaux Left, I kept hearing.

Which Left, which Left, came the reply.

No right ends on this team.

They were all lined up on the left.

Even the line was shifted left.

Linebackers, running backs, quarterback, all looking left.

Ball hiked into the quarterback's left hand.

Spinning left he threw a left turning spiral pass with his left hand and arm.

Perfect spiral.

Landing into the left arms of the left tight end.

Who ran to the left side of the end zone.

I was finished.

I had had enough.

It was tough to be tough all the time.

I headed back to town.

I thumbed a ride with my Left thumb, on the Left side of the road.

A Left Leaning priest stopped.

Opening his left window, he asked where I was heading.

Back to Town Left Square I told him.

"Get in," he said as he opened the left rear door.

Along the way he left me speechless with his allegories.

"Thanks," I said as I left him.

Walking up the stairs to what was left of my house, I opened the door to go in.

Time to relax.

I turned on the TV to watch an ultra-politically

Leftist commentator.

I dined on leftover pizza.

Drank leftover beer.

It had been a good day, and I was going to savor that part of the day that I still had left.

Notes (Lost Forever)

Thoughts jotted down
On paper.
So they won't get lost.
One got away!
Causing the biggest frown.
A mental crater.
Oh, at what cost?
Two on this day!!

Now needing to back track.
To find those lost thoughts.
Not on any paper.
Not in any note.
Pondering, thinking, are they tucked way back?
Connecting multiple brain dots.
Wait, is that a faker?
Did they drown in a mental, watery, moat?

Lost forever amongst new thoughts?
No longer in the forefront.
No longer a pressing need.
Did they retire to the note stable?
Tying your head up in the knots.
Semantic, gibberish stunt.
Lost to time and new note greed.
Becoming one more lost note fable.

Chocolate Snaccident

I was involved in a snaccident.
Night after night it befell me.
Excuses were so deja poo.
A right of atelophobia sacrament.
As bad as eternal perkatory.
The chocolate would moo, moo, and moo,

The snaccident came in many flavors.
Dark, milk, white, swiss milk, and even
Couverture chocolate.
Never time for a boregasm.
A tidsoptimist needing many flavors.
I would perambulate with an open wallet.
Hoping to dive into the chocolate chasm.

My livelihood no longer mattered.
Obsession to the point of becoming querulous.
Wandering the streets, I could only be veridical.
Searching, listening to the psithurism in the tress.
Head bent down, often burbling incoherently, my life was shattered.
Chocolate had become my sole lust.
Chocolate had become piffling political.

Chocolate was my new heroin.
I would even resort to defenestration for it.
I was fully aware of my occhiolism.
The world be damned, I was no humanitarian.
The sweven floated in my head for a bit.
Anxiously waiting for another to find this me-toosim.

The Right to Write About a Rite, Right, or Wright

Writing about the right rite.
The rite of writing.
I had to Google it, right?
Alas, Google had no rite of write or writing.
Perhaps a rite of right?
Struck out again.

My mind screamed.
There must be a rite of writing or a right to be right! (and to write.)
Google must be wrong. Or was it right?
Had spinning.
I must write about the right rite!
Not the wrong rite or the wrong right.
Perhaps a wordsmith or playwright could help with the right rite, or right, and
show me what to write.
I rightfully called my friend, Clark Wright.
He was always right, and right of right.

I was assured that I had a right to write about the rite.
If only I would turn right at Wright Street.
There I would find the Right building dedicated to the right right, or did he
mean right rite? Or so I was told.
I opened the right door on my car and drove away.

The Right building on Wright street was in shambles.
There had been a protest the night before about who had the right right, or
perhaps it was a right rite. I could not tell.

All that was left was the right wall, with an inscriptionon it
"Here stands the Right building on Wright Street, a place to write about the right, or the right rite, or even the wrong right. All who enter have the right to sit and write about any right or rite."

Leaving in dismay, I called Clark Wright.
He said I could write at his fishing camp on Right Avenue
located on Wright Lake.
There I found a bottle of just the right spirits.
By then my zest for writing had gone.
Instead, knowing that I could no longer write
about any right, Wright, or rite, I sat
for a long time
and consumed that bottle of right spirits to
calm the left side of my brain.
Right?

After all, I also had the right
not to write about any rite,
Wright, or right, right?

To Tion, Cian, Tian, or Sion
(That Is the Question)

Shall I be a noun?
Shall I be a verb?
Do I want communication?
Or do I seek to stand alone?

What do I do with gumption?
It does not fit the mold.
A tion that has been shunned?
A word in a world of its own.

Cian needs crea (tion) (Musician, electrician, magician, optician—those that create.)
It requires one or more to perform—like a beautician.
Tion needs its verbs (communicate, fix, frustrate, and more)
A symbolic rela (tion) ship?—words in herds?

Then there is the lowly tian.
Sounding like an Egyptian.
Walking like a Venetian or Martian.
Barking like a Dalmatian,
Speaking from Dalmatia.

I have a confession about an obsession.
An accommodation of a passion.
A magical profession…explosion, collision.
Sexual revolution…persuasion, compassion.

Growing Old

I forgot.
My mind said hello
But, I forgot
What it said.

Instead I looked outside,
Watching the hummingbirds dance and fly.
I forgot.
They were not there.

But then I thought
About stars, clouds and such.
The beauty of nature.
But, I forgot.

I forgot about today.
I forgot about you.
I forgot to forget.
Then everything was new.

Poems to Rhyme?

To assert that all poems must rhyme
One needs to take a long climb
Wading through intellectual grime.
Slogging along with gobs of slime.
Best to explore the issue in the daytime.
Not nighttime.
All the while watching how much time
You spend on this mental crime.
Poems have emotional enzyme.
They strike a chord in peacetime.
In wartime.
Or even in football over time.
Rhyme?
Nah, never, strike me down, but don't bother
me with it during lunch time.
Keep it less than sublime.
I'll take mine with tequila and lime.
Don't tell me that's a crime!

If I had 2 nickels, would I have a dime?
The bells toll, and my doorbell does chime.
I am hung up on brime (Guess that one.)
Sure wish I had penned this in my prime.
But rhyme? All poems must rhyme?
Nah, never, and especially not during Super Bowl half time.

Going Somewhere

Where, Ware and Wear were walking somewhere.

Not sure where, just somewhere.

While walking the three saw an invitation.

An Invitation to a coronation.

The coronation of their friend, Bubba.

Where and Wear knew exactly what to wear.

But what shall I wear?

Said Ware to Where.

Where shall I begin replied Where to Ware.

Where? Asked Ware.

Why start right where you can see the wear.

The wear from the tire tracks, that's where,

Said Ware

Ah, you mean over there?

Yes, over there, over by where Where is standing.

Ok, I got it replied Ware as he strolled over to Where.

And so it was that Where, Ware and Wear

finally got somewhere.

They followed those tracks to the closest store.

There, Where, Ware and Wear tried on everything.

But Ware was never satisfied with anything he could wear.

Since Ware could not make up his mind.

He decided to just go in his underwear.

I swear he was not bare, but that underwear.

It left nothing to the imagination.

You could see everywhere under there, under the underwear.

So it came to be that Ware became known as Prince Underwear.

To all his friends, to Where and Wear and to everyone else everywhere.

The end.

I Lost, Then Found a Friend

I lost a friend.
No, really, I lost a friend.
We were walking.
She was talking.
About something she wanted to lend.

We turned a corner.
And, proof, she was gone.
Maybe there was a dimensional border.
Perhaps she walked into a new dawn.

I looked everywhere.
Under a bench.
Under a chair.
In a bathroom full of stench.

I looked high and low.
I screamed at the top of my lungs.
I asked strangers about her red bow.
I felt like I was speaking in tongues!

I called her mom.
I called her dad.
Her mom started to recite a psalm.
Her dad laughed, he seemed glad.

Son, he said, that girl is a pro.
One moment here, the next gone.

She's done it to more than one beau.
Then he let out a long yawn.

Come back in about an hour.
She'll be here by then.
Probably have with her a bouquet of flowers.
And talking about you and other men.

As I was walking away, she came around the bend.
Where ya been I asked.
Remember that thing I wanted to lend?
We'll, I needed to be masked.

I put one on and you walked right on by.
Never suspecting that it was I,
I followed you around like a fly.
But, you never saw me in your eyes.

I appreciate you looking so hard for me.
That means a lot.
Would you like to come in for a cup of tea?
Your friendship is not for naught.

Odd, how friendships go.
But, so nice that they can sustain
The loss of a pro.
And rev up your happy brain.

This COVID stuff can be interesting.
Put a mask on and become a new person.
Even entrancing.
Especially when your friend with the mask
becomes your lover.

Maria

There once was a girl named Maria.
Her risqué photos appearing in every galleria.
She teased all the boys.
Saying, "I want to play with your toys."
Then disappeared after having a margaratia.

Young and Free

Yeah I am young and free.
But…this car is older than me.
No bucket seats!
No electric windows!
And look at that arm rest!
I am bursting.
And, if you look real close.
You will see.
No seat belt!
Now I am totally free!
Bam, oops, screech!

Of Love

Walk with Me #7

Through the forest of thoughts.
Along the blustering path of romance.
Up the winding trail of our lives.
Walk with me.

Travelling an uncertain road to parenthood.
Building each child as strong as can be.
Working to build castles in the sky.
Walk with me.

Watching loved ones pass into eternity.
While others grow and find their own paths.
Friends warming the trail.
Walk with me.

As time slips silently away.
Sometimes fast, other times slow.
Watching each other change before our eyes.
Walk with me

Is that me in the mirror?
All gray, no, white, with no more brown.
Skin dropping in places it used to be tight.
Walk with me.

After 40 years with one another.
Still enjoying a laugh, a quiet moment.
A longing and loving glance.
Walk with me.

Walk with me under the moon light.
Walk with me in the sweltering sun.
Walk with me onto the dance floor of life.
Walk with me forevermore.

Walk with Me #13

Wind in our faces.
Sun drenching our eyes.
The road lines keep us in our places.
Time flies.

Sweat rolling down.
Jerseys saturated.
Wheels spinning, spinning around.
New firsts created.

No walk today.
Instead, we ride.
Two bikes screaming down the highway.
Father and son keeping pace, stride for stride.

Walk with Me #20

He was a desperado for love.
Walking on emotional nails through hailstorms, tornadoes, and floods.
Dreams came to him in broad daylight.
Storming into view, searing sun bright.

She was serenely confused.
Walking a tightrope of frustration.
Sick and tired of being excused and emotionally bruised.
Depending on her work for elation.

They were not supposed to ever meet.
But fate intervened—the meeting was discrete.
A friend knew them both.
The meeting happened—emotional growth.

Eyes met eyes.
Words entangled with words.
Smiles opened up spectacular skies.
No denying—the two were their own rewards.

One complimented the other.
Conversation flowed seamlessly.
Together they could go so much further.
Hearts entwined peacefully.

But both had other commitments.
Mountains and valleys of resistance.
Religious obligations.
Deep, deep family foundations.

Daily duties, daily struggles.
More and more troubles.
Never a moment of peace.
Lists of things to do that would never cease.

Caught in the whirlwind of daily life.
An artist's rendition with pallet knife.
An oil painting smeared and messy.
It was so much easier to play the heavy.

So they wondered about what would never be.
He as he traveled, at least in his mind.
She as she watched her children, her family tree.
Together from afar—their love blind.

A chance meeting, an evening romance.
It happens all over the world.
Romance in a smile, in a momentary glance.
Romance that ends for better or worse in a land
of dreams, in a line or a phrase, in memories
that are hidden and never to be unfurled.

Walk with Me #23

A window in your heart.
A fragile glimpse of your soul.
Who you really are.
What sets you apart.
What makes you whole.
What makes you a star.

Not the Hollywood kind.
Those are easy to find.
A dime a dozen.
They are good at bluffing.
Not an athletic superstar.
So many of them are simply bizarre.

Instead, the kind that works hard every day.
The kind that leaves no stone unturned.
The kind that stays in touch.
The kind who loves a little horseplay.
One who will not let you get burned.
A person you would call in a clutch.

The star who keeps their heart window on display.
Who lets you see their soul every day.
The one where character counts.
Never demanding a recount—or talking behind your back.
A rare breed.
Holding onto an even rarer creed.

I have met one or two or three.

On the road to eternity.

Under the Blue sky.

Without even having to try.

Just pure circumstance, pure luck.

Being run over by a joyous Mack truck—while on a walk through my life and time.

Walk with Me #29

In the darkness glows a candle.
Lighting a small section.
Taking you out of the darkness.
If not for a brief moment.
Carefully down your path you amble.
Finding a new warm connection.
A refuge amongst ravaging emotionless starkness.
A respite from society's endless torment.

Candles along your path gently light the way.
Giving light to others on their journey.
Letting you peer slightly ahead, slightly behind.
Human knowledge increased with each one.
Some heralding a brighter day.
Visions no longer so blurry.
Able to survive the daily grind.
Each step a new journey begun.

Candles of love.
Candles of joy.
Candles of friendship.
Small flickering warmth's.
Gifts from above.
Gifts from within.
Surfacing from the darkness.
Warming the heart's hearth.

Walk with any person.
Walk with any child.

Look into their eyes.
The candle is there to see.
Pull back your curtain.
Be not blind.
Your candle—part of the skies.
Your candle, come walk with me.

Walk with Me #38

Long ago I walked alone thru winter.
Believing in only myself alone.
Then I came upon a face radiant!
Changing my life with a smile and a wink.
Forevermore would I be lost in love.
Not wanting to ever lose her ardor.
Living every moment with such delight.
Lying awake every night listening.
Dreaming of moments, future true events.
With her alone in love's embracing songs.
Working together amongst the blue sky.
Running through flowering fields of heaven.
Rolling tenderly together as one.
My eyes touching her eyes, her soul, and more.

The Rocking Chair

Made in an old Cajun's workshop.
It was nothing spectacular.
Plain wood.
Simple stretcher supports from one leg to another.
The rockers as straight as they could.
But the best that could be done by that Cajun cutter.
Four rails, all straight, for the back.
The cowhide seat was secured with many a tack.
The rear legs and stiles were round with a bauble at the top.
The front legs were essentially the same, but without the top bebop.

It had seen 4 generations of children.
All rocked with the greatest care.
The art of rocking and sleeping it knew well.
No child ever had to despair.
It had multiple stories to tell.

One time it saw the birth of a child.
Waiting patiently in a corner unseen.
Struggling with each birthing groan.
Making sure it was immaculately clean.
Waiting to rock the new milestone.

Derbes rocked on it during cochon de laits.
As the pig roasted for hours by the hardwood fire,
The kinfolk danced and drank the hours away.
Never minding the smoke or sweet scent and never seeming to tire.
Waiting expectantly for the marinated, pit—roasted, young, suckling pig,
sliced thin and served with gravy.

Riding on Mardi gras floats conveying an elder,
Listening to the bands play their tunes.
While the ladies showed their breasts and called for beads.
It loved the colorful costumes, beads, and balloons
All the while caring for its rider's needs.

It knew the Joie de vivre.
It reveled in Laissez les bons temps rouler.
It knew every Cajun dance
As well as the songs.
It was accustomed to the young ones taking a chance.
Not worried about any wrongs.

It was also there during many illnesses.
Helping the young and the old.
Rocking its soft song into the still night.
Waiting as long as it could to finally be told.
Of a victory or the loss of the fight.

It continues to rock with the present generation.
Taking on the scent of multiple owners.
Waiting to be handed down to the next.
By its present owners and donors.
It moves from one generation to the next with no personal effects.
But if you look or listen closely you will find.
All the stories wrapped up in its plain wood lines.

Compassion

Walking hand in hand.
A simple squeeze conveys countless messages.
Making each feel secure.
At that moment and beyond.

An elderly couple teetering down the hall.
Helping one another attain their mutual goal.
A mother with child in a wheelchair.
Her smile so pure, loving, and serene.

A family of three sipping on coffee or tea.
Speaking in low tones as they exit the hospital.
Two gents discussing the prognosis.
Of whom I know not.

So ironic that in a place of sickness, pain, and death,
Compassion wells to the surface.
Becomes so apparent.
For everyone to see.

Laughter reverberating from each wall.
Someone expressing joy.
Speaking to someone on his cell phone.
Heading to the elevators to go upstairs.

A mother with a young boy in a wheelchair, sleeping.
Turns my way and our eyes meet.
A smile instantly tells me of the love between the two.

They stop, linger, look in the gift shop window and continue their stroll down the hall.

All the while the young boy sleeping.

Hugging your sister for a long, long, time.

Saying, "I love you."

Knowing she is in a fight for her life.

Engulfed in the cancer battle.

She whispers back, "I love you too."

Siblings

Crawling, standing, running, and jumping.
Learning new tricks every day.
Fighting, squabbling, over what TV channel to watch.
Protecting each other when there is no other way.

Making up excuses when getting in late.
Making sure your stories are straight 'bout that last date.
Sharing a car with two or three others.
Not necessarily all brothers.

Knowing each other's inner most desires.
Helping one another climb intellectual spires.
Cutting you to the quick with a simple comment.
Momentarily making you feel despondent.

Watching as the others mature and leave you behind.
Each one in turn learning to flex their minds.
Struggling with maturity and responsibility.
Achieving goals with versatility and humility.

Growing old together even if at a distance.
Reconnecting via a path of least resistance.
Again laughing, cajoling, and reminiscing.
As if you were never missing.
Siblings are to be treasured.
They are never to be measured.
Siblings are one of a kind.
Never to be maligned or left behind.

Her Love for You

She walks toward you.
Her footsteps quiet, determined and strong.
The smell of her coolness enveloping the room.
Coming ever so close as if the words of a love song.
Ready to surround you with her scented perfume.

She reaches out.
Touching your arm as well as your soul.
Touching your heart with her sweet, sweet, smile.
Making it apparent that you are the goal.
Willing to undergo the harshest trial.

She surrounds you with lush smells and desires.
Making you lose all consciousness.
Your ego flies ever so high.
Sailings softly through unconsciousness.
Returning to reality at the sound of her sigh

She wraps you in her arms.
You know what to do.
The touch of her lips against your cheek.
Makes you fall thru.
To the next level of reality.

You return her passion.
With the touch of your hand.
Against her fair breast.
Warming your soul like the desert sands.
Flying together to an unspoken penultimate crest.

She lays you gently down
Beside her with a sparkle in her eyes.
Her love she bequeaths you.
It is as splendid as the blue of all the skies.
And as one you are born anew.

Love and Friendship

Scents of Summer Breezes.
Lingering around the nape of her neck.
Glistening drops running down the curve of her spine.
Falling into soft curves.
Not adhering to any sort of gravity.

Running hand in hand.
Laughing together at the wind and the sky.
Speaking in secretive tones
About nothing in particular.
Wondering…is it time?

Softly falling into space.
Dancing as one.
Knowing a perfect moment.
Never to be replaced.
Waiting for the brush of her cheek or the touch of her hair.

Lovers or friends forever?
Watching her eyes to see if there is more.
Feeling her touch from miles away.

Passing time in a lonely state of mind.
Laughing at a silly rhyme.
Decisions determine fate for the two.
Star crossed friends or Lovers, closer than two drops of dew.
Friends becoming Lovers and Lovers becoming friends.
Love and friendship intertwined forever.
The two parting never.

Run Away with Me
Let's Be Runaways

Run away with me.
If not for real, then in my imagination.
If not for fact, then in a sweet, sweet, dream.
Run away with me right now.
Run away with me to set us free.

As the hummingbird flies from flower to flower.
Let us leave our humdrum lives behind.
Let us live for today and tomorrow.
Let us leave the past to others.
Run away with me in a warm summer shower.

We can fly to New York.
Stay for a week or a day.
We can stay at the Whitby, just blocks from Central Park.
You will love their gardens.
The flowers speak of your smile.

We can sail to London Town on the Queen Mary.
Dancing the night away.
Sunbathing in the Atlantic Sun.
Enjoying a meal of Salmon Gravlax with Poached Quail's Egg or a Croquette
of Suckling Pig
Cruising to our destination.
I can see the sun reflecting off your soft, dark, hair.

The Cotswold Hills are calling us.

Above the Severn Valley and Evesham Vale.

We can stay at Ellenborough Park.

Or we can catch a brew at the Porch House and stay in one of their quaint rooms.

The choice is yours.

Your eyes would sparkle and shine.

Paris is just a stone's throw away.

We could dine at the Eiffel Tower, Jules Verne restaurant.

During the day we could pretend we were Parisians and blend in at Fouquet's Café on Champs-Elysees.

The curve of your legs fitting perfectly under the outdoor table for two.

Run away with me.

Leave it all behind.

Let's winter in Moscow.

We can stay a month or two.

Hotel Baltschug Kempinski is just a block from Red Square.

We can attend ballets at the Bolshoi Theatre.

You can wear a golden sable fur coat, with a Russian Fox Fur Hat.

Your breath would form snowflakes as we walk along.

Moscow in the winter with you.

Run away with me.

Budapest, Cairo, Istanbul.

We can stay at them all.

Lounging in a hammock at the Bora Bora Nui Hotel.

Watching tropical fish float by.

Your sun-tanned body a work of art.

Run away with me.

Sao Paulo, Machu Picchu, and Rio.

We can stay there for a year for a rest.

Dining at Solar da Republica Lanchonete, Coffee Lab, or at the Urbe Café Bar.

In Rio it would be the Vizinho Gastrobar, Bar do Momo, or Pabu Izakaya for a change.

You could wear traditional Chilean clothes.

We could ride burros from town to town.

Run away with me.

Let's leave our responsibilities behind.

Let's run with the setting sun.

Let's swim in every ocean and sunbathe on every beach.

Let's hike in all the mountains and climbs to the Earth's highest points.

Let's walk down famous avenues and eat in famous bars.

Run away with me.

A Kiss

A kiss placed lightly on your cheek.
With sudden warmth and passion.
Finding your soul.
Openly, and then gone.
With stealth, so to speak.
Gently, but with passion.
Not sure of its goal.
A true phenomenon.

There are other kisses.
A mother's kiss.
Reassuring.
Ever so kind.
As you leave for school.
Helping you on your way.

A sister's kiss.
After not seeing you for months.
A welcome back kiss, if there ever was one.
Sending you back to your childhood days.
Letting you know that you are not alone.

An aunt's kiss.
The one's you try to avoid.
But still kind.
Even if you get annoyed.
Try not to mind.

A father's kiss.
Letting you know he is still there.
A listening ear.
A thoughtful voice.
Helping you with many choices.

But, none compare to that soft touch with passion.
The one that sends your head spinning.
The one that invigorates your imagination.
That soft touch on your cheek.
The one given with compassion.
The one that speaks to a beginning.
The one that begs for a longer duration.
The one that makes it impossible to speak.

In the Long Run

No one ever taught me how to write a poem.
Yes, there were high school classes.
Where teachers taught like they were on loan.
Some ideas presented as mere flashes.

Then I experienced loss.
It was the hardest and cruelest teacher.
Loss of one near and dear.
Loss of a friend.
Loss that was impossible to toss.

Somehow loss also taught joy.
And taught the value of laughter.
Taught just how to deploy.
Words that would go here, there, and even thereafter.

Putting down a thought or a feeling.
In a sentence or line.
Capturing the moment as it was squealing
For a brief moment in time like a disposable shrine.

My poems still have much to desire.
There is still a fear
That the words might invoke some to conspire
And hurt some held so near and dear.

Some lines can have multiple meanings.
Most are simple and plain.
Words that float apparently dreaming.
Of awakening in others thoughts like drops of rain.

Urging them to think
To go beyond their quiet and safe realm.
To take a peek and then rethink.
Just exactly who is at their helm.

No one ever taught me how to end a poem.
But loss taught me how to abstractly kiss someone.
Even though not present they can be hugged with thoughts.
And that often has to do in this life in the long run.

Lovers Delight

Perched safely in the sky, planets fly by.
Partners circling slowly, a dance of love.
Dancing around the sun so royally.
Each with stories subtle to our bare ears.
Venus, goddess of lust, hot with desire.
Mars, full of anger, ready to wage war.
Mercury, circling fast on winged feet.
Saturn with her lovely rings, keeping track.
Many the topic of poet's creations.
Lover's wishing on one every warm night.
Eternal wishes on pure, welcome lips.
Lover's arms, space entangled, orbiting.
Breath hotter than Mercury's scorching air.
Circling, wondering, unspoken delight.

Pure Delight

A mother's delight.
Love's purest scent.

Forevermore

The sound of her voice gently wraps itself around your heart.
Caressing every fiber, never wanting her to depart.
Shaking your innermost foundations.
Thinking of new, vibrant, ecstatic, creations.

As she approaches it becomes clear.
Her presence will always be near
to your heart, your soul,
While on your life's stroll.

Something in her eyes.
wakes your soul to a new sunrise.
The touch of her hand
makes you understand.

A beacon of light
in your personal night.
A song of compassion
dressed in simple fashion.

You sit for days on end
Praying that her voice she will send
A small token, a brief spoken line.
Something, anything would be fine.
Long standing, emotional connections
needing no spiritual corrections.
Even from distances afar

Small words are better than some forgotten memoir.
She glides through the air,
never disturbing a single hair.
Walking on a silvery cushion.
On a singular mission.

You want so much more.
A stroll on love's seashore.
A secret, fleeting, kiss would do.
Anything from her to you.

Nothing in the universe like it.
A singular fireball of emotional grit.
Packaged in something so fair.
Catching you unaware.

Warmth, intellect, strength, wrapped inside.
Streaming through her eyes, emotions collide.
No escape, none wanted.
Needs silently expressed in every breath.

Shakespeare, Byron, could never describe.
the grace, warmth, beauty she held inside.
You want nothing more.
than to be with her forevermore.

Chefs

Save room for dessert.
Save room for the main course.
Save room for the hors d'oeuvre.
Mix them up.
Salads for the extrovert.
Soups for the man who is hoarse.
Cocktails for those who serve.
We can all be chefs in this lineup.

Chefs feed the person.
Chefs feed the soul.
Chefs help lovers love.
They mix up relationship's brews.
Like a fine bottle of bourbon.
Letting you sink your soul into the worldly casserole.
Helping others taste life's Club sandwich.
Getting drunk on relationship booze.

Simply sitting with another for a fantastic meal.
Brings conversation out like tossed salads.
Romance as hot as a baked potato.
Lovers as spicy as a well stuffed jalapeno pepper.
Good food helps seal the deal.
Adding a special touch to lovers'pallets.
Chefs adding to the lover's dough.
Helping couples condense like good cheddar.

Ah, desserts of life.

Desserts of food.

Desserts of the spirit.

Desserts of love.

Chefs at relieving strife.

Chefs helping us become emotionally nude.

Poets with a different kind of floret.

Philosophers that understand life's most tasteful doves.

Dreams

In my dreams I run away with you.
We dance on a bridge in Central Park.
Nature's architecture surrounds us.
Human architecture in the distance.
I twirl you left then right in the morning dew.
Igniting an eternal spark.
To some an affair.
Treasonous.
To us—coexistence.

The world twirls around.
On its axis forever bound.
The stars light up the sky.
Points of love for lovers this night.
For us no worldly bounds.
Everlasting lover's sound.
Emotions soaring as high as they can fly.
Reaching ecstasy's height.

In my dreams we never part.
Dancing in Central Park
until dawn.
Dancing into eternity.
Dancing for the love of one another.
In my dreams you are always in my heart.
Never, never, to be gone.
In my dreams we fit perfectly.
In my dreams there is no one else to discover.

I Heard a Bird Chirping

I heard a bird chirping.
Singing its beautiful song.
Strong, pure, full of vigor.
It stayed outside my window for so very long.
Telling me that your soul had taken flight.
That the skies were so beautiful.
You had become a song.
A thing of absolute beauty.
Not to worry.
That you were free at last.
I heard a bird chirping.

Dancing on a Dime

One soul sitting in a cafe.
The other hopping out of a pickup truck.
Not knowing the closeness to come.
She walked in.
An air of familiarity.
Eyes of strength.
The music began
Slowly, in their souls.
A glimmer at first, a crescendo later.
In the air a nearness, indescribable.
An invitation.
An exchange.
Instant kinship.
One moment leading to years of intimacy.
A moment lasting.
A closeness increasing.
As if on a crowded dance floor.
So intertwined, they were dancing on a dime.

Love's Reach

Gently, oh so gently, the waters of our life touch Love's beach.
After so many years, our glasses looking empty are so filled.
Life's adventures, memories filled, within love's reach.
The fruits of our labors, the view we have, we willed.

Etched Hands

His hands held secrets inside each deep line.
Her wrinkles, smooth so many years ago, knowing.
Thousands traveling the same road sublime.
Millions gone to the gusty wind growing.
Billions of loving thoughts drifting ever skyward.
Lessons taught, retaught, handed from wise bards.
History etched deeply in each forehead.
Eyes having seen a thousand new sunrises.
Experiencing wars, poverty, love.
Surviving illness, births, death, and more.
Finding smiling faces along the way.
Smiling with love on the growing, new, young.
Time growing short, but still so much to do.
Without regret soon fading slowly away.

Tear

Tear of love.
Tear of grief.
Tear of joy.
Tear of relief.
All rolled into one.
When you said we were done.

Bridge Between Us

The bridge between us.
Family waters flowing underneath.
Obligations to children, spouses, others.
Skyscrapers of daily undertakings.
No time for us to even discuss.
No chance to even breathe.
Society, religious norms, did smoother
Any chance to express strong feelings.

So you stayed on your side.
I stayed on mine.
Never meeting in the middle.
Viewing each other from afar.
Finding ways to emotionally hide.
Enjoying small talk via internet poetry lines.
Sending back and forth cryptic riddles.
Still wishing upon a star.

You peeked.
I peeked.
But, we never sneaked.

Emotional View

Standing before you.
Peering deeply into your eyes.
Winds of emotion float through my mind.
Deep, deep feelings for you.
Listening for any signs or sighs.
Reveling in my find.

Standing beside you.
Facing the world together.
The sprouting of new emotions every day.
Each a new challenging view.
Never uttering the word whether.
Knowing we will find our way.

Standing behind you.
Watching you effortlessly stride.
Emotion's song swelling in my heart.
Your presence a savory roux.
With nothing to hide.
Each of us playing our part.

Dancing through life with you.
The flowering of intimate emotion.
The deep lines of secrets bonding.
Still sending me a clue.
Forming emotional notions.
Your touch…my responding.

The Moment of Intimacy

A mother's first view of her baby.
A father's first chance to hold the child.
More than a chemical reaction.
Beyond a visual experience.
A feeling of utter, sublime safety.
Souls reconciled.
Not a human abstraction.
Glorious.

The moment you say, "I do."
While peering into your lover's eyes.
A gentle, long hug.
From someone struggling.
At that moment you knew.
Never wanting everlasting goodbyes.

L'instant d'amour.
Experiencing extreme emotional, spiritual, closeness.
Vivre une extreme proximite spirituelle emotionnelle.
Love.
Lust.
Something needing strong boldness.

A glance.
A momentary romance.
A wish, a longing for more.
I saw you…

A night in Paris.
Dancing together in a trance.
Perfectly paired.
We knew.

Closeness.
Familiarity.
Affair, Amour.
Liaison, Affection.
Sensuality, Tenderness.
Steps to those moments of intimacy heaven.

Loves Heat

Heat of my day.
Streaming from your inner sun.
Clouds gone.
Clouds of distrust gone, too.
The touch has much to say.
No place to run.
Sensuality with an earthly tone.
Driving away everything blue.

Heat of my night.
Descending from the lover's moon.
Tearing at my soul.
Inflaming desires.
Eyes searingly bright.
Smile beckoning…come soon.
Hands…cool celestial poles.
So many sensual fires.

Heat of my heart.
Every entangled breath.
Effortless compassion.
Continual bliss.
Every morning a new start.
Waking passion.
Passion that never quits.

Heat of my dreams.
Forever more.
Never parting.

Coloring my world.
Love's many-colored streams.
Each smile opens doors.
Each hug disarming.
Creating our own dream world.

Light Softly Rising

The light softly rises each splendid morning.
Rising slowly, perfectly, without speed.
Finding its place in each person's being.
Warmth emanating from its very deep core.
Your light should also rise each awesome morning.
Waste not the warmth emanating from you.
Your warmth, your light, shines upon every soul.
Placed here not to hide, but to soar so high.
Warmth and light, a gift bestowed from above.
Carry them forward to your many loves.
Let them bask and grow as seedlings rise up.
Justice and humanity cry for it.
Light, warmth, embodied gracefully in you.
Share those qualities with those around you.

Thoughts of You

The thought of you
Used to make me fly
So high.
Now, I sink from view.
My sound now a sigh.
As thoughts of you go by.

Rise Up

Beautiful flower.
Waste not gentle power.
This your hour.
Rise, do not cower.

Winter Dampens Not the Spirit

Winter days grow long, testing life's meaning.
Cold winds chill the warm hearth of young lovers.
Souls gather round fond tables quelling its hopes.
Its goal, extinguishing spiritual norms.
Coming veiled with pretentious glowing smiles.
Alluring Sirens with beautiful song.
Hoping to dash young spirits on cold walls.
Mighty sailors braving torrid north winds.
Sailing for their distant far off home ports.
The songs of winter winds troubles lost sorts.
The spirit nestled inside each warm heart.
Shielded from winters cruel heartlessness.
Peers beyond, gathering love's finest art.
Finding strength to brave mean winter's cold dart.

A Sister Lost

Confusion, consternation, disbelief.
Life gone…a wisp of fleeting, tumbling smoke.
Rising into majestic, blue relief.
Suddenly, one true voice no longer heard, felt.
Listening…perhaps still in the wind, sky.
Amongst tall trees, flowered fields, mountain peaks.
Soft music, raucous rock, sultry jazz…there?
Between pages of a book, lines of poems?
Shadows of spinning bike wheels…a voice felt.
Sounds of tires on the road…her chorus true.
Climbing another hill, another peak.
Climbing ever higher to heaven's great heights.
No pain any longer, just majestic grand rides.
Lost amongst clouds, stars…the beautiful new sights.

Doors

Your life so full of opening shut doors.
Ones that remain locked to so many ears.
Ones that are closed to so many eyes.
The doors that seem so solid like huge rocks.
Carved from granite, marble, or cold ice.
Doors that have haunted your childhood young years.
Mysteries behind each and everyone.
In shadows they remain, biding their time.
Needing a light and love to be opened.
Once opened so many sights to right behold.
The other side illuminating much more.
Looking back, you wonder about it all.
The doors, the light, the laughter, and loves all.
Doors no longer shut, now open as meant.

For You

Thoughts of you.
Scattered between realities visions.
Briefly coming into view.
Serene smile.
Gentle laugh.
Dancing eyes.
Compassionate, clear, voice.
Stately composure.
Then receding.
Dusty memories.
Shortly gone.
Reality beckons.
The daily grind calls.
Rising again ever so often.
But less and less.
The dust obscuring the view.
The view of you.

Unlit Love

Pity the soul that has no love.
Cold days.
Sterile nights.
Dreary autumns
Somber springs.
Wasted summers.
Icy Winters.
No love from without.
No love from within.
No hands to hold.
No feet to tickle.
No cheeks to pinch.
No lips to kiss.
Pray they find a way.
To meet another.
Have a simple conversation.
That warms their soul.
Stokes their fires.
And let's them join the human—race.

Cold Passion

Cold passion surrounds me.
Only warmth from myself…
Since you have been gone.
Your loss has blinded me.
Adrift in this emotionless sea.
Singing a blue song.
Return and set me free.

Two Smiles

The sun never sets.
The moon always in the sky.
Beams of love surround them.
Two smiles.
Two innocents.
Making the world a better place.

Sunday Morning

It was a sultry Sunday morning.
Windows dripping in sweat.
Coffee aromas called me from my slumber.
Hearing soft humming from the kitchen.
I sauntered quietly down the hall.
Then, swiftly placing a warm peck on her neck,
She turned, half eaten doughnut in hand.
Gave my hand a squeeze, a loving smile.
Revealing her delights.
Only for me to see.

Pink with sprinkles.
Chocolate delights.
Frosted for fun.
Chicory coffee.
Donuts of delight.
All on a sleepy, sultry, Sunday morning.

Of Spirit

Walk with Me #8

Casting stones.
Sheathed in false knowledge.
Directed at no one and everyone.
Debris fall all around.

Broken sprits, broken lives.
A pittance, don't look back.
The view strangulated.
Selfishness wins the day.

Walk through large crowds.
Infect them all.
They are nothing
After all.

No feeling, no remorse.
Cold, cold, heart and mind.
Let them die.
Let them wither on the vine.

You dare not walk with another.
Compassion might sneak in.
Loving another
Should be a mortal sin.

Engulf them in fire.
Take their breath away.
Leave them limp, cold.
Fixed eyes.

Listen not to any healers.
They give too much hope.
Card dealers.
Walk with me, I am death, despair, depression.
Walk with me and lose all hope.

Walk with Me #9

Walk with me on the sands of time.
Let it wiggle between your toes.
Feel it ripple in the waves.
Observe it in the shells we find.

So much to show you.
So many things to teach.
This beach is our classroom.
Countless lesson for your growing mind.

Walk down here while the water warms our feet.
Feel how it comes and goes.
Innumerable thing in life do the same.
As we pass on through.

See that colorful shell.
Rings from small to big.
Growth is for all living creatures.
From flower's seeds to flowers, from babies to adults.

Ah, a piece of drift wood, all weathered and dry.
Much like your Poppy.
All life change as it ages—God made it so.
No science has been able to stop it, no matter how hard they try.

Look, a school of fish.
Small, darting from here to there.
Together for protection.
I wonder if they know how to wish.

As they grow they will go their separate ways.
So it will be for you and your friends.
Friends grow and find new paths.
Family will always be here.

Observe the sand crab.
Scurrying from hole to hole.
It knows it is small.
Ducking for protection.

We too must learn the art for protection.
Needed as we grow.
Instincts honed.
As we strive for greater perfection.

Watch the dolphin and her young.
Teamwork as a family.
Teamwork as a group.
The many helping each other.

The beach and it's many occupants.
A cast like no other.
And, yet, like so many others.
Eyes open, ears listening, take it all in.
You may never pass this way again.

Walk with Me #16

An eternal fire swirls around us—and through us.
No eye can see it.
No skin can feel it.
It does not burn.

But it is there.
No human can control it.
No science can bottle it.
If you reach out you can sense it.

For those that seek it, it offers protection.
But it does not beckon to be sought.
No one knows it's exact location.
With it you can feel whole.

A flickering flame that each soul is born with
No need to wish—it is a gift.
A flickering flame that shines in the dark.
Many have described it—without ever having seen it.

We know not it's goals—except eternity.
The flame can paint.
It can sit and wait—for a long, long time.
The flame can sing—you can hear it in the wind.

Some repress the flame—do they feel shame?
Some deny it exists—but it persists.
Lost, but to be found.
Eternal patience.

Walk under the sun.
Walk under the stars.
Walk in the rain.
There, did you glimpse it?

Walk with Me #17

Courage under the fire.
Another cancer victim.
Thrown upon that vicious, unholy pyre.
Thrown out of life's rhythm.
One more tragically stricken.

Acute lymphocytic leukemia.
Acute myeloid leukemia.
Chronic lymphocytic leukemia.
Chronic myeloid leukemia.
Hairy cell leukemia.
Myelodysplastic syndromes.
All out to rain on someone's parade.

Treatment from hell.
Dark, dank, dungeons in the bright, sterile, rooms.
Nurses and doctors, purveyors of pain.
Hoping for a cure—that makes it right.
Hardly able to stay sane.
All a great bane.
Enjoy your lumbar puncture.
Relish the bone marrow biopsy.
Drink or inject that chemotherapy cocktail—hmm, so good.
Lie still for your radiation tan.
The bone marrow biopsy needle is such a delight.
Go ahead, kick some sand.

Pray that you don't get sick.
Your body's immune system destroyed.
Pray for a stem cell transplant.
Pray that your lungs stay healthy.
Pneumonia will make you pant.
Infusion of red blood cells to help your power plant.

Lines leading from this arm.
More from the other.
Lose your hair.
Lose your vision.
Lose your will to survive.
But fight on, the only chance to thrive.

Walk with a cancer patient, for a moment, for a day.
Feel their grief, experience their anguish.
See their bravery.
Watch them fight, and fight to stay.
Then you will know why some of us pray.

Walk with Me #24

Walk with me, I am twenty-six years of age.
Not many years on this earth.
But enough to see my mother die.
Enough to turn an emotional page.
Old enough to understand birth and rebirth.
Wise enough to know when a doctor must lie.

Barely along my path of independence.
Still finding my living balance.
Searching for stability in this insane world.
Not wanting to understand transcendence.
Never having experienced unchained malice.
Eyes not wanting to see anything so gnarled.

I remember the call.
My mind raced, my heart sank.
Your voice so calm.
I clutched the wall, preventing my fall.
Words unspoken.
My world shattered—emotional fragmentation bomb.

I was your only child…
At the age of twenty-six.
A special bond between mother and son.
Emotions, events, that would take years to be reconciled.
I had seen the world through your eyes for so long.
Now your eyes would be gone forever.

Words no one should have to hear.
Words that strike, strike, and strike fear.
Words that make you grow up so, so fast.
Cancer, leukemia, time is drawing near.
Wishing that past days could last and last.
Place them in a bottle and hold them to your breast.

Traveling home at breakneck speed.
Seeing your smile.
Hearing your voice—it will be alright.
I can get a bone marrow transplant.
But in the end, it was not to be.
Fate had other plans for you and me.

The downward slide came faster and faster.
Ah, two months of respite.
Then downward again.
Nothing able to stop the slide.
That horrendous ride—into oblivion.
My eyes watching as you slipped away.

Holding hands.
No more surgeries, no more horrors, no more pain.
The smile on your lips.
The love in your eyes.
There until the last breath.
Then peace at last.

I will always be twenty-six.
I am frozen in time.
My heart will always yearn to hear your words.
My eyes will search for you in all the crowds.
My life will go on.
But, I will always be twenty-six.

Walk with Me #30

I came upon a linear leaf.
Thinner than an ovate one.
An elliptical one crossed my path.
Oblong leaves sang in a choir.
Cordate leaves were sopranos.
Altos were the reniforms.
Obiculars comprised the baritones.
Cuneates made up the bass trio.
Rhomboids, spatulates, obliques, hastates sat in the audience.

They came in all sorts of colors.
Generally, all starting out green.
Even the acicular ones.
Like the heart of a child, no matter their place on this earth.
Then as they matured.
Some turned red.
Some turned orange.
Some turned yellow.
Some turned brown.
But within, the sap flowed the same.

I came upon a thin man.
Thinner than an oval one.
A bouncy lady crossed my path.
Chunky men and women sang in a choir.
Thin lipped girls the sopranos.

Kidney shaped woman the altos.
Odd-shaped heads sang baritone.
Men with wedge shaped bodies the bass section.
Diamond shaped, spoon shaped, begonia shaped,
double ear lobed people made up the audience.

They came in all sorts of heights.
All starting out small.
Changing as they grew.
Life's lessons changing them all.
Then as they matured.
Some turned red.
Some turned orange.
Some turned yellow.
Some turned brown.
But within, the blood flowed the same.

I came upon a leaf.
I came upon a boy.
I came upon a man.
I came upon a girl.
I came upon a woman.
I came upon the world as I walked down my path.

Walk with Me #39

I walked alone, along a darkened road.
No goals, no signposts, no spiritual load.
I proclaimed to all I met that I was absolutely free.
Nothing holding me back, there wasn't anything I couldn't do or see.

I met a stranger on that road.
He had multiple scars that showed.
I asked him about his afflictions.
He answered with sincere convictions.

The scars had been self-inflicted.
During a time in his life when he was drug addicted.
He smiled, sheepishly, and told me.
That he could see that I wasn't really free.

I asked him how he could say that.
Then on the ground I spat.
Easy, he responded.
You remind me of me.

I used to wander these roads, alone like you.
Searching for the latest thrill.
Never thinking of the bodily toll, just about the next party or one-night screw.
Then the needle I found, thought it was new.

A needle in my arm.
I thought I was a charm.
I could feel no harm.
To me the needle did not alarm.

Little did I know.
That the needle was robbing my soul.
My life filled with woe.
My mind like a tossed salad bowl.

I wandered the roads just like you.
So full of myself.
Pretending never to be blue.
Only thinking of fun in and of itself.

My parents, siblings, and friends were all idiots
I knew better than all of them.
That were simply parrots.
Espousing the latest societal phlegm.

I never took the time to look inside.
I never thought of my own pride.
There were plenty that saw it my way.
With them, I learned to stay.

Then one day, upon waking in a gutter.
With only one shoe on and freezing to death.
A single person dropped down to me and said with a mutter.
You are lost, but you still have spiritual breath.

Follow me for a day or two.
I will feed and clothe you.
Then you can tell me to go screw.
If you still feel blue.

Heck, I had nothing to lose.
I was already at the bottom of my luck.
How could I refuse.
Shoes, clothes, and some food…I was stuck.
We didn't walk far.
We didn't have to.

Instead, he pointed out this bird, this insect, or this star.
Then he asked if I noticed anything new.

I wasn't sure what he meant.
But, I was intrigued by spiritual breath.
Maybe it was the way he would vent.
Or perhaps that meaning deep underneath.

Possibly it was the food we ate.
It might have been from staying up so late.
But something changed in me.
I no longer needed the needle or any magic tea.

We sat in his simple camp for three days.
Eating, sleeping, and talking about the many ways.
Ways to care for ourselves and others.
Ways to shelter sisters and brothers.

On the fourth day he was gone when I woke.
He left me a short note.
It simply said, "Treat others
the way I have treated you."

So, stranger, I make this offer to thee.
Spend some time with me.
I'll feed, clothe you, and give you a place to rest.
Ya ain't got nothin' to lose, this ain't no test.

If after those three days you still want to throw your mind, body and spirit away.
I won't get in your way.
And I certainly won't stay
I took him up in this offer and walked his way.

After those three days he went his way.

I went mine.

I won't tell you the result of that stay.

But, I will ask you to stop a moment and with me pray.

Freedom

Freedom has a few good expressions.
Words as you want to use them.
Music you want to hear.
Paintings you want to see.

The sky, clouds, flowers, and greenery are your paintings.
The wind in your ears the music.
The chatter of your wheels the words.
The road, path, or trail, your freedom.

Freedom to see, smell, think, and feel.
While rolling along.
In a sprint, up a hill, or lazily down the road.
Choices are endless.
Visions countless.
Words enumerable.

What lies beyond that hill?
The smell of spring?
Sunshine or rain?
The downhill rush of excitement?
Like diving into a cloudy pool of water.
All senses alive, yearning, burning.

Some race to satisfy a need.
Some cruise to satisfy a desire.
Other tour fast or slow, months at a time.
All are hooked.
Fascinated by the freedom that cycling brings.

Humanity

Humanity walks down a path.
A path with thousands of twists and turns.
Venturing sometimes with eyes closed.
Sometimes with a cold heart that burns.
Often with bare nerves fully exposed.

Other times it is a good Shepherd.
Caring with all its might for what is best.
Taking steps positive and true.
A path that will not rest.
Taking us far beyond the morning dew.

How long can humanity exist.
Will we reach the stars?
Are we fated to hate one another?
Can we learn to be sisters and brother?
Taking time to cherish what is momentarily ours.

Will religion be our doom?
Can there be no room for more than one?
For thoughts and feelings that differ.
As long as they do not hate, maim, or kill.
Can they be tolerated with no ill will?

The birth of a child.
The love of two people.
Gives hope to those who feel exiled.
Under any sky, roof, or steeple.
For the continuation of our species on its celestial path.

Our galaxy is old.

It turns ever so slow.

Two hundred and fifty million years per rotation.

Humanity has been a brief, bright, glow.

Located on a blue ball in constant motion.

Wandering through the halls of space and time.

Never completely knowing its destination.

Never completely knowing if it has a place further down the line.

Pilgrims, One and All

A Pilgrim.
Cultural pilgrimage.
Political pilgrimage.
Religious pilgrimage.
Tourist pilgrimage.
Educational pilgrimage.
Sexual pilgrimage.

One and all.
We are all travelers seeking.
Happiness.
Liberty.
Freedom.
Equality.
A chance to bask in God's sun.

One and all,
We wander in our thoughts.
Imagining better times.
Repeating scenes of joy and wonder.
We wander in our daily lives.
Struggling from day to day.

One and all.
We walk in foreign places.
States of mind.
Expressions of emotion.
Artistic renditions.

Various devotions.
Trying to be kind.

One and all—
We journey through our lives.
Side by side, dancing together.
Crossing paths.
Never meeting or knowing one another.
Lives, short or long, important to others.

One and all, we are pilgrims.
Of some sort.
Sailing in the Milky Way galaxy at a million miles per hour.
Never felling that speed.
The distances too great to fathom.
Faster than any phantom.

One and all—
We live and we die.
We love, hate, cry, laugh, and rejoice.
In our own fashion.
We make friends, then watch them leave.
Their growth down another path.

Through countless generations, pilgrims we have been.
Persistently seeking.
Each person their own mission.
Even in love the individual soul continues.
But sharing the pilgrimage.
With another can open your eyes even more.

One and all.
Pilgrims we have been.
Pilgrims we are.
Pilgrims we shall be forevermore.

There Is a Reason

There is a reason.
Sometimes we don't know why.
But there is a reason.
For everything that flies by.

There is a reason.
For the drunks in the street.
For the children with bare feet.
There is a reason for every season.

There is a reason for the child born today.
A reason for a laughter and joy.
It might be hard to see.
But there is a reason for love to exist.

There is a reason.
I can see it in your eyes.
Not to hide any lies.
To let the truth shine through.

There is a reason.
For us all to exist in this place and time.
It is hard to know why.
We have to try so hard during our climb.

There is a reason.
Perhaps it will always be unknown.
But, perhaps all will be revealed some day.
Perhaps when humanity has grown.

To a point where it can understand the true reason we are here.
Without hatred, dread, or fear.
There is a reason.

Ghosts Walk Amongst Us

Most do not believe in ghost.
But I do.
They walk amongst us every day.
Silently, or not, sending us messages.
Some prophetic, others not.

Columbus walks amongst us.
Sending the spirit of exploration.
Telling us to search the unknown.
Reminding us that the journey will be hard.
But not to waiver.

Washington walks amongst us.
Reminding us of freedom's delicate nature.
Teaching us to stay the course.
Not to waiver.
That freedom needs protection.

Jefferson walks amongst us.
Speaking of saving the Democracy.
That manifest destiny comes with a price.
A price that must be paid.
That freedom is a God given right to all people.

Sitting Bull walks amongst us.
Teaching us that no government is perfect.
That as a people we must control the government.
And not the government the people.
That it is the people who form the more perfect union.

Mahatma Gandhi walks amongst us.
Making us recognize how to transform a nation.
As others did, to take down a tyranny.
Without firing even a shot.
But with patient determination.

Rachel Carson walks amongst us.
Still speaking of the silent spring.
Urging us to be good Shepard's of God's green earth.
Teaching us the art of investigation.
To speak when words need to be spoken.

Henry Ford walks amongst us.
As does Thomas Edison, and countless inventors.
Calling on the human spirit to prevail.
To shine a light into dark places.
For the better of mankind and the world.

These ghosts and so many more.
Trod this earth every day.
You can see them in most everything you do.
In every place you go.
In everything you hold dear, and say.

Standing Still

I ventured down a path.
Through a field of green.
It meandered a bit.
Coming to an intersection, initially unseen.

It was a crossroads.
The path turned right, left, and went straight.
I stopped and stood for a long, long, time.
Considering all my tomorrows.

I could go left.
I could go right.
I could go straight or turn around.
I thought about what would be best.

Then I realized there was another path.
The one that said stay.
Go no further.
You can stand still and let others pass.

All that time I thought I was alone.
On a path for one.
Instead, it was travelled by many.
So, I built a cabin at that intersection.

Then others came to pass.
Coming down the right or left path.
Coming from ahead or behind.
They all had to come by my dwelling.

I could learn what was up ahead or behind.
By inviting them in.
Through simple interaction.
I could do this and not be blind.

And so it was.
For me standing still—
Let me find so much and so many others.
All that from a simple pause (and reflection).

First Light

Birds chirp and sing.
Frogs croak.
Crickets harmonize.
Crows caw.
World coming alive.

Squirrels bark.
Gnats appear from their slumber.
Egrets soar to their feeding spot.
Sky lightens.
Gray becoming blue.
Soft light touches your eyes.

Breezes speaking of spring.
Cool to the touch.
Gently caressing your cheeks.
Hints of summer in those winds.
Swirling lightly, hints of rose.

Scents from the ground.
Scents from the flowers and trees.
Heavenly sent.
For you.
For me.
The world found.

Bees attend to business.
Lights appear in dwellings.
Human activity.

Sun emerges, breathtaking.
The world is alive.
Listen, see, smell.
A new day arrives.

Some Words

Some words were only meant to be written.
Other words were only meant to be spoken.
Some were meant not to be uttered at all.
Carefully choosing not to be bitten.
Responsibly chosen so friendship will not be broken.
Deciding which to avoid so that you will not fall.

There are times when you want to retract what you have said or written.
There are times when words simply will not do.
This darn digital age can so easily put you out in the shed.
So hard for those to be unwritten.
In the end making you so blue.

Damn the words.
Perhaps my lips should be sewn shut.
Perhaps my pens should be forever banished.
Words were not meant to be a house of cards.
Words were meant to open doors.
Words were meant to elevate and open one's heart to be astonished!
Words are alive, they can grow and grow.
Words are yours to sow.

Silence

Silence pervades the clamour.
Listen for it between the rising voices.
It calls to be heard above all the racket.
Calming in its many choices.

Sometimes you can hear it between pundit's sentences.
It is there amongst the shoes shuffling down the street.
You can find it between the parentheses
On a singer song writer's music sheet.

Silence above and mixed into the din.
Sweet, sweet, silence as fragrant as any rose.
Existing just below societies blaring skin.
Search for it in life's meadows.

The brother and sister of tranquility.
Breathing hope into those who despair.
Take a moment and try it to help rid hostility.
In its own right important enough to share.

Two souls enjoying silence.
A third can easily join in.
A multitude helps create balance.
Be still, learn to contemplate, listen to what dwells within.

Almost a Human Right

A pair of slippers, pajamas, and a robe.
Hard to beat on a cold winter night.
Something so common across the globe.
Worn by kings, queens, and commoners at twilight.

Settle into the warmth of the layers.
They are yours, not the public's.
Slippers, pajamas, your robe, and your prayers.
Your smells, your curves, your own republic.

Light the fire.
Turn down the lights.
Settle into your evening attire.
Relax and go over the day's highlights.

Just you and your loved ones.
Not many people get to see your evening clothes.
The clothes that are worn by most everyone,
But not to Broadway shows.

You spend lots of time in those pieces of evening attire.
Sleeping in the pajamas most every night.
Most might have just one or two that they wear.
In the summer they tend to be light.
Pajamas, slippers, and a robe almost a human right.

In the winter they keep you warm.
In the spring they can help keep out any residual cold.

In the summer they are your evening uniform.
In the fall they become a part of your household.

But all in all, they are our evening dress.
Used time and time again.
A time to relax and remove the daily stress.
The evening armor removing the daily pain.

So special.
Important to human refreshment.
A time for those awake to settle.
There for your nightly protection and reflection.

Peace of Mind

Peace of mind comes in many forms.
Sitting in a rocker on the back porch, watching the birds fly by.
Listening to a song, current or from days long gone by.
Just as long as the moment is not torn.

Practicing a slow breathing technique.
Easing your mind.
Being kind.
Down dog, spinal twist, doodle bug or even happy baby are fine.
Helping leave the world behind, even if for a moment making you happy.

Watching grandchildren run and play.
Speaking in low tones to a loved one.
Making it all a special day.
Not wanting it to ever be done.

Riding a rollercoaster for a thrill.
Eating cotton candy at a fair.
Even a precise, exact military drill.
Peace of mind can be found just about anywhere.

No person, no family, no nation owns it.
Instead, it blows in the wind to all who would seek it.
A moment of bliss, an hour of joy.
Peace of mind can come in the form of a child's simple toy.

Nor religion, no philosophy, has a lock on it.
Like freedom, it knows no boundaries.
Seek it for your pleasure.
Bask in it for as long as you can for your leisure.

Blue Skies

I dream of blue skies with wispy clouds.
I dream of rainy days with a cooling wind.
I dream of open roads without the city crowds.
I dream of curving roads and scents of summer downwind.

The scent of spring.
The heat of summer.
The inevitable sprint and sting.
Coming upon a newcomer.

The relish of the tailwind.
Making dreams come alive.
The pain of the headwind.
Enduring the headlong drive.

Dressing for the cold.
Taking off layers for the heat.
Decisions on comfort can be bold.
Shades with different lenses are sweet.

Deciding what path to take.
Shall it be left or right?
A multi-day tour on the make.
Right this time and riding into the night.

Unloading the gear and setting up the tent.
A nightly ritual that is so sublime.
Out in nature, exactly where you want to be sent.
No worry about the next day's climb.

Cooking over a campfire or camp stove.

Eating under the stars.

No blaring TV to ruin your man-made alcove.

No fumes from the tailpipes of congested cars.

Oh, to be on the road.

To go for that multi-day spin.

Leaving for one more episode.

Living the luxury of freedom away from the city din.

Dreams can come alive.

Planning for the future ride is part of the fun.

The ride is something for which to strive.

The first turn of your pedals, and you are gone like a rabbit on the run.

Truth or Lies

Does any good come from morbid subterfuge?
Do we gain when deceit controls our days?
Shall we become prisoners to confuse?
The fox with hens has its monstrous ways.
A dog in heat can easily diverge.
Running in circles as others delay.
Can a lie smoothly spoken become true?
Heard by so many unsuspecting ears.
Held so close, accounting for many fears.
Corrupt men and honest men wear like shoes.
Silver tongues are born every single day.
Finding ample room on life's long highway.
Those who would govern the day can be long.
If they govern from the throne of strong wrong.

Freedom's Wind

Shhhh.

Listen.

Freedom's wind glistens.

Soul Mask

Look past the mask.
See the eyes.
There the soul survives.

Day's End

Sun setting.
Rays warming spots on the trees.
Temperature dipping.
Egrets flying home for the night.
Birds chirping their evening songs.
Fish surfacing for one more bite.
King snake snoozing in a hole by the dock.
Light fading.
Candles lit on the table by the water.
Sipping an evening drink.
As the world settles down.
Slipping into its sleeping bag of night.
No breeze to be felt.
But cool, crisp, evening air.
No TV noise.
No Facebook chatter.
Crickets slowly calling out.
Frogs seeking one another.
Soft hoots of owls out and about.
Nature resetting for the next day.

A Walk-Through Louisiana

The land of hurricanes, sultry summer days.
The land of swamps, alligators, and cotton mouths.
The land of magnolia trees, egrets, and the mighty Mississippi.
I sing your praise.

The home of the Blues, Creole Zydeco, Dixieland jazz and Cajun (old French) music.
A mixing pot of African, Creole, Acadian, Isleno cultures to name a few.
Catholicism, Southern Baptist, Pentecostal,
Methodist, Jewish, Mormon, Muslims, even Atheists have a place here.
Cotton, corn, evergreen trees, rice and crawfish are some of your crops.
Your might mixes show your diversity.

Fighting Tigers, Jaguars, Grambling Tigers, Ragin Cajuns, Warhawks, Bulldogs, Cowboys, Green Wave, Privateers, Colonels, Wildcats, are a few of our college football team.
Musical legends, Louis Armstrong, Lil Wayne, Fats Domino, Dr. John, Aaron Neville, Mahalia Jackson, Harry Conick, Jr. all call Louisiana home.
Justin Wilson, Paul Prudhomme, Herman Perrodin, Austin Leslie, Emeril Lagasse, Charles Henry Brandt, John Folse gave our food to the world.
Cajun spices: Slap Ya Mama, Tony Chachere's Louisiana Cajun Seasoning, Zatarains, Richards, Perique Pepper sauce, Comeaux's Cajun Carole seasoning, Cajun Chef, and McIlhenny Tabasco sauce, all from this wonderful state.
My senses, my ears, herald you.

From the French Quarter in New Orleans, to the Red River District of Shreveport, to the Biedenharn Museum & Gardens in Monroe, to the Kent House Plantation in Alexandria, to the Lake Martin Rookery in Lafayette, to the Creole Nature Trail & Adventure Point in Lake Charles, we have diversity of towns and nature.

The cultures are just as diverse: white, black, Asian, Mexican, heterosexual, LGBT, cyclists, runners, swimmers, walkers. We have them all. Truck drivers, electric car drivers, SUV drivers, foreign car drivers, yes we allow them too.

Snow in the winter you can find in the north, ocean breezes around Grand Isle, bass biting in Toledo Bend, deer jumping in the Kisatchie Forest, spring and fall is glorious, growing vegetables all year round.
Your glories to be explored.

Your people know how to celebrate life.
Mardi Gras a state wide delight.
Festival International de Louisiana draws many in.
Breaux Bridge Crawfish Festival a party to behold.
Bogalusa Blues and Heritage Festival not to be outdone.
Ponchatoula Strawberry Festival will wet your pallet.
Even the Franklin Parish Catfish Festival is a cause to celebrate.
Ah, Louisiana, you know how to glorify life!

A state that has known many nation owners and the land of many Indian tribes.
The site of the earliest known Indian mound site in North America.
Poverty Point reaching its peak in 1500 BC.
Indians known as Alabama, Koasati (Coushatta)
Choctaw Jena, Bayou Lacombe, Clifton,
Chitimacha, Houma, and Tunica—Biloxi. A mix of Choctaw and Apache groups rounds out your Indian heritage.
Spain, France, Great Britain all had a role.
Germans settled along the Mississippi River in an area called the German Coast just above New Orleans.
Haitians joined your culture and brought some of their own.
Finally becoming a territory of the USA in 1803.
Louisiana, a true mixing pot.
Louisiana, I trumpet your past!

John Ruddell of Tulane University invented the binocular microscope; the Multiple-effect Evaporator used in water desalination invented by Norbert Rillieux; the Sazerac a true Louisiana drink; the first Opera in our country held in New Orleans.

John James Audubon, E. J. Bellocq with his ladies of the night, George Rodrigue with his blue dog, Clementine Hunter with her views of Louisiana life, Gertrude Morgan with her outside life, Robert Malcolm Rucker with his outside landscapes.

James Carville with his political comments, John Kennedy with his one liner wit, Edwin Edwards who went to jail, Huey P. Long who would put a chicken in every pot, Russel Long who served in the senate for so very long, a long list of charismatic Louisiana politicians.

No story would be complete without a listing of some desperate minds: Madame Delphine La Laurie—prominent New Orleans socialite who kept her slaves in a torture chamber; Stanley Tookie Williams—one of the founders of the West Side Crips in L.A.; Lee Harvey Oswald—killed President John F Kennedy; Charles Matranga—Founder of the New Orleans Mafia in 1870; all called Louisiana home at one time or another.

Louisiana, I raise a glass to your ability to endure.

Through all sorts of weather, you have learned to persist.

Great Mississippi Flood of 1927—The worst river flood in U.S. history; Mississippi flood of 1973—Affected areas around the Mississippi River in Louisiana; May 1995 Louisiana flood—much of New Orleans flooded after heavy rainfall across South Louisiana; 2005 Levee failures in Greater New Orleans—After Hurricane Katrina; 2011 Mississippi River floods. Severe flooding across the Mississippi River Valley; 2015 Louisiana floods—the Red River reached record levels; 2016 Louisiana floods—Prolonged rainfall across south Louisiana caused catastrophic flooding resulting in over 146,000 flooded homes and 13 deaths.

Louisiana, I shout your resilience and resolve to the heavens.

Cajun, Creole, Country, Cowboy, Bible Belt, Oil Roustabouts, Black, White, Asian, Mexican, French, German, English, Arabic, Syrian, South African all add to your splendid mix.

Louisiana, a land to be explored.

From natural sights to man-made locations.
From beauty of the eye, to the joys filling ears.
From scalawags, to politicians, to religions of all sorts.
From senses that fill your taste, fill your eyes,
Fill your ears and satisfy your soul.
A place to rejoice about the diversity of life.
A place to take a long, long walk.
And realize that you are not alone.

The Decline of the Search
for the Truth

Democracy, they say, is the governmental form of the Search for the truth.

Socrates is often described as the father of western philosophy.

A searcher for the Truth.

A questioner of everything.

The Grecian cities of Athens and Sparta the sparks.

Poor Socrates was eventually tried, and killed by hemlock.

Perhaps he asked one too many questions.

Perhaps the leaders of Athens did not care about the truth.

He is credited with saying, "I am the wisest man alive, for I know one thing, and that is I know nothing."

And "there is only one good, knowledge, and one evil, ignorance."

In today's modern America we are at a crossroads.

Citizens now belong to 'epistemic tribes': one person's truth is another's hoax or lie.

No one is right, no one is wrong.

Everyone is right, everyone is wrong.

Truth be damned, truth chained to a tree.

When did it start? Are we destined to fail and fall?

It seems that our politicians have forgotten that they serve the people.

So many simply try to get rich.

Throwing the rest of us into ditch.

It seems that they all just want power.

Perhaps with Nixon, perhaps with Clinton, perhaps with Bush, perhaps with Obama, perhaps with Trump, perhaps with Biden.

Does it really matter? The truth dies nonetheless.

Animal Farm in reality. "All animals are equal, but some animals are more equal than others."

1984—Thought crime, Thought police, Newspeak, Crimethink.

Are these the new Norms?

1984—"Now I will tell you the answer to my question. It is this. The party seeks power entirely for its own sake. We are not interested in the good of others; we are interested solely in power, pure power."

Have all our political parties succumbed?

Does no one seek the truth anymore?

Is it just a money game?

Has the individual died?

The media has gone insane.

All forms of yellow journalism now exist.

They used to seek the truth.

But now, it eludes them.

Take a side, they all seem to say.

They need to stop and take a look.

They need to ask hard questions of every politician, not just the ones they dislike.

We need the media to help search for the truth.

Not their truth, but the truth.

Without them the people have few protections.

We need a return to Socrates.

Admit that you know nothing, then every question opens up.

Quest for knowledge, quest for truth.

Our democracy depends on it.

The Roman Empire Lasted for over 1000 years.

Shall we?

"To find yourself, think for yourself," said Socrates.

Words as true today as way back then.

Open your eyes, open your ears.

Seek the truth.
Be not afraid.

Ignorance comes in many forms.
It hides around every corner.
Asking you to blindly follow, and not question anything.
I saw it in the banning of books.
The adventures of Huckleberry Finn, Of Mice and Men, the Color Purple, A Wrinkle in Time, To Kill a Mockingbird, Animal Farm, 1984, to name a few.
Books that expand the mind and asked the reader to ask questions.
Books that made you realize that "Education is the kindling of a flame, not the filling of a vessel."

I wish we could all be like Socrates.
Asking probing questions.
Our leaders be damned.
They need to answer to us, the people.
Again and again.

Brewing Storm

On the horizon.
Over some hills.
Past some mountains.
Views allegedly brighten.
Speeches from word mills.
Sounds of cannons.

Rolling thunder.
Crash of lightening.
Pounding of hooves.
No one admitting any blunder.
Quite frightening.
Counting the number of approves.

Wolves openly parading.
Labels their disguise.
Tearing away all fabric.
Ripping, biting, marauding.
Everyone cries.
Rolling out a new tactic.

Words describing.
Adjectives, adverbs, drawing swords.
Twenty-four hours a day.
Freedom writhing.
Cities big chessboards.
Waiting on the next play.

Horizons grow darker.
Fires stoked.
Lines forming.
In the eyes of the archer.
Everyone provoked.
Prophecies swarming.

Nature and mankind colliding.
Humans wrestling to the death.
Political views butting heads.
Humanity backsliding.
Gasping for fresh breath.
Liberty at a crossroads.

Some watch from outside.
Others in the mixing bowl.
The batter being swirled.
A few have seats ringside.
The rest performing within the storms howl.
In the balance, the free world.

Storms brewing on multiple fronts.
Sleeping giants.
Sleeping no more.
Coming over the horizon all at once.
Causing untamed riots.
Pushing society to the brink of oblivion's seashore.

First View

The primordial being awoke.
And feeling the universe's wind said, "Let me have eyes.
I must see where that wind came from."
So it was, and so it shall ever be.

I Wonder

When I look up into the skies, I wonder.
Who am I?
What am I doing here?
How far away is that star?
Why does the sun keep us warm?
What is the age of the universe?
Are we alone?
I wonder.
And I wander.
My thoughts drifting from question to question.
Then there is you.
And of that, I do not have to wonder.

Society's Sages

Unsteady gate.
Knees constantly hurt.
Pain shooting into the left big toe.
Mechanical chairs to get up.
Vision failing.
Hair falling.
Selective hearing increasing.
Fingers stiff.
Skin dropping.
Turkey neck.
Flapping arms.
Memory stuck in the 60s.
And yet, you are society's sage.
An elder to be respected.
Keep moving.
You ain't done yet.

I See a Bright Future

America, that shining star in the west.
From early times
Even before Europeans arrived.
Glimmered with natural promise.
Vast prairies, open skies, mighty rivers.

Some say America has seen its best day.
That its fires are being extinguished.
To them the sky is always falling.
O, those fires with might still roar.
Time has not diminished them.

The industrial revolution continues.
Perhaps in different ways.
Steamships being replaced with electric cars.
E-mail replacing the electric telegraph
People adapt so rapidly to the change.

America still shines, still burns brightly.
Still the beacon of freedom for the world.
Individuality not snuffed out.
Creativity, ingenuity still rewarded.
People able to follow their dreams.
Hard, tireless effort still required.
Taxing fortitude and intellect daily.
Success is not handed out, it is won.
Rewards through hard efforts…the prize.
Seize the day, run with the sun.
We have sent humans to the moon.

We will see it again, and Mars.
The fires burn strong and bright.
Personal computers invented here.
Roaring with ingenuity might.

Weed Wacker, yes, Wacker, now for everyone.
O, those weeds have never experienced such might.
Whacking weeds everyone's delight.
Email close behind, now used by the masses.
Inventive fires a Human right.

We all drive, some have more than one car.
Anti-lock brakes, for going near and far.
Our lives could use some brakes these days.
Video games first invented here.
Magnavox Odyssey started the craze.

American creations continue to thrill.
Tesla, MRI machine, Fit Bit, but a few.
So much to be proud about.
In this mixing pot, this American stew.
No intellectual drought.

Our future is ours to decide
The American sprit still taking a wild ride.
From sea to shining sea.
We ride the fires of creation at high tide.
For all to rejoice and see.

Found

I was high.
I mean I was f…ing high.
Stumbling high.
Incoherent high.
Mumbling high.

Walking, meandering down the road.
Head sunk deep…heavy load.
Stinking of booze.
A real hophead toad.
A stoner goat.
Always sozzled and stewed.

He came around the corner.
Sandals, blue jeans and a dirty T-shirt.
He looked me straight in the eyes.
I stopped, he stopped.
Then he spoke, sounding like one, but no stoner.
Not a bong rat, cooker, or cracker convert.
Nor a starch shirt business type wearing ties.
Still, someone who had not flipped or flopped.

He said, "Dude, where ya going?"
"Down the road, dude," I spat.
"Hey, can I walk with ya for a while," he responded.
"It's a free country," came my response.

So he turned and walked with me, I could of sworn he was glowing.
Then he asked, "You high as a black cat?"
I stopped, astounded.
His stance so nonchalant.

"What's it to ya?" I spewed.
"You a cop, or a narc, in disguise?"
"Nah. I just didn't meet any stoners my time here before."
"I'm still learning about this world as it ages."
I didn't feel pursued but confused.
He didn't look at me like I was some prize.
Certainly, I wasn't his chore.
His look so contagious.

Then he did something real cool.
He offered me a salami sandwich.
The kind my mom used to make.
So we walked, I chewed, he talked.

He wanted to know how long I had been a cool fool.
If I had ever run with many bandits.
Whether I had ever tried to drown in a lake.
It was strange, but I was not shocked.

He seemed to fit right in.
Or at least grasped my sin.
He wasn't afraid, no fear in his eyes.
He smiled as we talked that afternoon.
Me, the junkie, him with the grin.
As I started to come down, struggling within
He just kept talking, looking into the skies.
Never treating me like a f...ing buffoon.

He told me there was plenty of room for my kind.
Kind of shocked me, I always thought I was toast.
Never went to a dance.

Never wore any fancy clothes.
Always grinding that daily grind.
Dreading the next day's clucking roast.
Waiting for some whore to give me a glance.
Up my nose, or new lows, who knows.

And so it went that day.
Back and forth, time slipping away.
But that glow stuck in my mind.
I know what I saw.
Somehow it was gone, that feeling of doomsday.
My need to be tanked, thrown under the bus on the freeway.
My thinking, less clouded, more streamlined.
Someone actually sat and spoke with this outlaw.

He indicated it was time for him to go.
He stood up real slow.
I, too, was ready to leave.
He grabbed my hand and gave it a friendly shake.
I could see the glow travel up my arm.
Darn it was warm.
"Remember me," is all he said, and adjusted his sleeve.
With that he walked on and I was fully awake.

I headed back to my crib, my home, my dive.
Unable to get him out of my mind.
He had treated this stoner kind.
Unsure if I wanted to use El Diablo again, you jive?

I ain't close to perfect, having lived so long in the zombie beehive.
But, darn, what a find (or was I the find?)
Heck, I even found a job and joined humankind.
And somehow started to feel alive.

(Why does he eat drink with sinners and publicans? And Jesus hearing it, said to them, "The well need not a physician, but the ill, I came not to call the righteous, but sinners.")

(And Jesus rising up and seeing no one but the woman, said to her, "Woman, where are those your accusers? Has no man condemned you?" And she said, "No man, Lord." And Jesus said to her, "Neither do I condemn you; go, and sin no more.")

Excerpts from the New Testament

Idiot's Paradise

It has me again.
The shakes.
Mind racing.
Tied to this chain.
The shakes is all it takes.
The abyss I am facing.

Sublime serenity on the other side.
For an hour or a day.
F…the world.
Rubber tubing, the ring of my bride.
The heated spoon, yeah, that's my way.
Ah, sweet syringe, fist tightly curled.

Heat of the rush.
Explosion in my mind.
Now sinking.
Yeah, man, you cool, just hush.
You sorry you declined?
Hot shit running down my leg, stinking.

F…, too much again.
Struggling for a breath.
Hey, man, can you help me stand?
Screw 911 man, they ain't messing with my brain.
Gimme some meth.
That will help get rid of this fairyland.

Just stay with me man.

Don't leave me alone.

Man, I am really blown.

Hope old man death looking in some other can.

Hope the cops think I be flown.

Shit, hope I can score so I can sit on the throne.

Don't mess with my head.

Hell, man, I ain't dead.

Maybe the kids need some food.

But, f…, I need some more to get in the right mood.

Shit, I think my heart just stopped.

Ah, F…, my time just popped.

Tap, Tap, Tap

Tap, tap, tap
Are you there?
Tap, tap, tap.
Can you hear me?
Can you see me?
I'm right over here.
I'm looking over your shoulder.
Looking in your eyes.
I can see your breath.
I can feel your heartbeat.
Your scent so enticing.
I am beside you every day.
In every way.
Waiting for the end of your stay.
Tap, tap, tap.
Waiting patiently.
I knock consistently.
Tap, tap, tap.
But you are not ready to let me in.
So, I wait.
I've got lots of time.
In fact, I've got an eternity

Guitar Life

Life is like an old guitar.
You are often:
Battered, scarred, discolored, wrinkled.
But you can still play a tune.

Lost Livelihood

I lament those who used to ride the rails.
Freedom's free riders, one and all.
Not a penny spent.
To get from here to there.
Working when they could…a kind of bail.
Bail to leave drudgery life, standing tall.
On those rail cars there was no rent.
Vast skies, open field, space to share.

Catching that slow moving train.
Moving from town to town.
Working along the way.
Just to move again.
Freedom's sugar cane.
Box Car Joe never had a frown.
T Bone Slim wandered many a day.
Throwing off society's chains.

Utah Phillips' songs about the rails.
Ran for President he did.
Do Nothing Party in 1976.
Connecticut Shorty a famous female rider.
A No. 1 (The Rambler) knew all the trails.
Writing 12 books about the hobo grid.
Yearnings they did stir.
Drinking freedom's hard cider.

Nowadays, punks, anarchists, crusty kids ride.
Hobo behavior codes broken.
True hobos now a rare breed.
A return to the old a grand need.
Hobos work and are respectful to every side.
Other's feelings not mere tokens.
Helping others in need.
Not out for materialistic greed.

Ride your life's train respectfully.
Make your own work if you can't find any.
Remember, your actions leave a legacy.
Most of all, remember to always be friendly.
While hobos might be a dying breed.
You can still live by the hobo's creed.

Time

Time bends.
But does not break.
Peeking at the future.
Time sends.
Not knowing what is at stake.
Not caring about nature or nurture.

Time can heal.
Broken hearts do mend.
Friendships reignite.
You cannot steal.
Comprehend?
Days dull, days bright.

Time at home.
Time at the beach.
Time in the snow.
Crafty magical gnome.
A growing pretty peach.
Lover's after glow.

Time surrounds.
Time binds.
Time destroys.
Finding happy hunting grounds.
Sometimes it grinds.
Sometimes it annoys.

Time in multiple disguises.
Clowns, criminals.
Cats, canines.
Any surprises?
Seemingly immense or minimal.
Aging like fine wines.

Time mixes with everything we do.
The living, the dead, the inert.
Never discriminating.
It never dies, never catches the flu.
Always, always, it's will to assert.
Never, never, ever waiting.

I Cried

Lover, I cried.
and heard nothing.
Lover, I cried
and saw nothing.
Lover, I cried.
and tasted nothing.
Lover, I cried.
and smelled nothing.
Lover, I cried.
and felt nothing.
Death was upon me.
Lover, I cried.

Twisting Moments

Anticipatory hesitation moments.
Between then, now, and to be.
When the mind changes direction.
Conscious but unconscious.
A delicate balance on a razor thin edge.
Enter indecision or decision.
Enter doubt or vision.
Enter time, yes, time.
A moment between human quests.
A time so small it is rarely noticed.
But there, nonetheless.
A blink.
A wink.
A fluttering ripple in your day.
With nothing to say.
But so much a part of your way.
Twisting in your mind.
Unconfined.

Creation

Subtle brush strokes of the mind.
Illuminating thoughts from within.
Molding ideas into real form.
Some cruel, some kind.
Some thrown into a trash bin.
Others becoming trumpeting horns.

Perhaps on paper.
Or in a womb.
In a galaxy far, far, away.
Seen or hidden in reality's vapor.
Ready to bloom.
Standing still, or willing to stray.

What form shall you take today?
Two eagles dancing in the sky?
Children creating their own world of entertainment?
Clouds parting for a sun's intense ray?
A movie camera into your world it might pry?
A moment of peak attainment.

Creation is all around us.
All the time.
In innumerable forms.
Songs of joy heard on a city bus.
At the scene of a sickening crime.
Stretching society's sometime not so solid norms.

Three children painting a picture.
Taking turns painting on one page.
Ya never know what you will see.
Perhaps something like an evil lamp fixture.
Or a lion in all its rage.
Maybe a swarm or one bee.

It never ends.
Day or night.
Cold or warm.
It has many close friends.
Some dull, others so, so bright.
But all helping humanity to come in the from the storm.

Touring

Simple things.
The turn of your pedals.
Shifting gears.
Watching the trail ahead.
What each day brings.
Testing your mettle.
Erasing fears.
Part of your life thread.

Clouds in the sky.
Cooling breezes whistling past.
Sunshine peeking out.
Warming your soul.
Serenity without having to try.
Quiet peacefulness that can last.
Stillness with a gentle clout.
Quietude the goal.

Away from the clamor.
Into the heart of nature.
We ride in the moment.
Savoring each second.
Leaving for days society's awful sledgehammer.
Cycling's portraiture.
Society's din broken.
Cycling's blessing.

Balance

Humanity encompassed in equity.
Emotions, action entangled in soft symmetry.
The need for parity in everyday encounters.
Beyond the flesh level, a need for inner harmony.
Sometimes long, sometimes expressed with brevity.
Flowing from one to another, such brilliancy.
Daily seen in nature's elegant flower.
Balance at the macro and micro level, such artistry.

Compassion

Compassion
That moment when someone kisses the hurt.
A brief gesture of deep love.
Different than, but like passion.
Sometimes feeling as similar as an old nightshirt.
From deep inside or from above.

Compassion.
Knowing when to lay down your arms.
A feeling passed from one to another.
Itself on a spiritual mission.
Protecting many from emotional harms.
Noticed in the eye of a sister or brother.

Compassion.
A divine human quality.
Seen in good times and bad.
The opposite of division.
A moment of intimate honesty.
Seen in good times, but also times sad.

Compassion.
Rooting out, expelling heartlessness.
Bringing forth a warm glow.
Often out of fashion.
Gently changing moments of callousness.
Humanities chance to shine and spiritually flow.

Skies

Skies of Wonder.
Wondrous skies.
Sky of blue, gray and white.
Skies of calm.
Calming skies.
Skies of rage.
Raging skies.
Ever peering downward.
Downward peering.
Since the dawn of time.
Time's dawn.
Oh, if you could only speak.
What stories you could tell.
Skies of life.
Living skies.
Skies of grief.
Grieving skies.
Skies of death.
Deathly skies.
Skies of warmth.
Warming skies.
Skies of love.
Loving skies.
Skies of every thought and emotion.
Earthly, heavenly, skies.

Grace

Grace comes silently, softly, from above.
A dove lighting on your shoulder.
Mercy, pardon, a second chance to Love.
A light feeling, an aura in the eyes of the beholder

Not just from the heavens.
But also a quality imbedded in many.
Seen in human acts of kindness.
Pouring from some like sweet honey.

But not just embedded.
Also seen in how some walk.
Grace and stature wedded.
Walking the walk and taking the talk.

A courtesy here, a favor there.
An act of mercy anywhere.
A quality that you can teach and share.
Grace…found so often in simple prayer

Spring Air

The grip of the depths of cold, cold, winter.
Leave with gasping sprinter hesitation.
Opening the way for breezes milder, soft.
Bringing with them scents new and decades old.
A hope, a wish for warmth from the tired cold.
Rays of sunshine beating back the dark clouds.
Cool breezes with hints of thinning cloud crowds.
Clover sprouting from between blades of grass.
Inviting busy bees from their winter hives.
Egrets, shinning white, floating in the skies.
Smells of lilacs, dogwoods, the earth plowed.
Spring air in all its majesty, so proud.
Take it all in while you can each new year.
Spring…relish it with dance, music, love, song!

Birthday Ride

Four for a birthday ride.
Starting out, knowing the goal.
No hurry, no worry.
Glide into the ride with pride.
Your bike meshing with your soul.
No time for the blues or being dreary.

Heading out with a tail wind.
Always a good sign.
Steady pace, staying together.
Ready for the uphill grind.
Watching for a chasing canine.
Feeling as light as a feather.

Twenty miles in, pick up the pace.
Not a race, so do it with style, grace.
Chatter as you ride…
Turns the ride into a glide.
Wheels humming in the wind.
Wheels, sun, wind, chatter, all intertwined

Sixty-three miles, plus a few more.
Darn, we can still turn those cranks.
Maybe a tad slower than in days gone by.
But, heck, at 63 this evens the score.
One more ride in the tanks.
One more ride under a beautiful Louisiana sky.

Society's Bane

We see it so often.
Another story hitting the late-night news.
A comment, underlined, in a newspaper story.
He fell from glory.
She fell into the afternoon blues.
Both sealing themselves in mental coffins.

It spreads across all races.
It dances across all party lines.
It claims both rich and poor.
You probably know a few faces.
You may have seen the signs.
Calamity washing upon the human shore.

New forms seem to pop up every day.
Taking our best into the unknown.
Destroying families, communities, and more.
It seems we have little reaching say.
It seems that heaven has taken a break…flown.
The devil on the loose to settle a score.

Another gone from an overdose.
Another arrested for supplying the stuff.
Small potatoes when you consider who is really in control.
But, oh, so gross, so morose that lethal dose.
How did he or she reach that dramatic bluff?
Who is really to blame for that hell hole?

People make decisions to use drugs every minute.

Every minute of every waking day.

You see it at every level of society.

People in business suits, typical brutes, those who are astute.

Fathers, mothers with good jobs, captured by the drug way.

Those who practiced sobriety, piety, succumbing to the notoriety.

Let's blame the parents.

Didn't they fail in guiding their offspring?

Shouldn't they have taught them how to sing?

Could the solution be that transparent?

They are a wellspring.

Influencing their young with just about anything.

Let's blame the schools.

Didn't we send our children there to learn how to stay away from the blues?

Weren't they supposed to spread the news?

Creating voices that can carry the news.

Teaching our children to avoid the drug bruise.

Teaching that to succeed you have to pay your dues.

Let's blame the politicians.

The ones who create our laws.

They needed to control this better, right?

Perhaps they need to view some bodies with the morticians.

Those laws are supposed to rid us of our flaws.

They are supposed to be helping us with all their might.

Let's blame the pharmaceutical companies.

They make the drugs.

The ones that end up on our streets.

Those subsidies they receive pure gluttony.

Money is all they know how to hug.

Extra dollars falling at their feet.

Let's blame the judges.
They let those criminals loose.
Instead of giving them the noose.
Out on the street to commit more crime.
Hey, bro, you got a nickel or a dime?
For a dime, I give you some good goose.

Drugs…man o man alive.
You ain't got no drugs, you ain't got no jive.
You got some drugs, lucky you still alive.
Some place we got on this earthly hive.
To survive today you got to contrive.
You got to stay in overdrive.
Toss that trash, find yourself a better way to survive.

Lache Pas La Patate
(Don't Let Go of the Potato
or Don't Give Up)

Darkness comes after daylight.
The night hiding many demons.
Demons disguised as sheep.
Speaking sweet, sweet, words into ears.
"Shhh, quiet now, have no fears.
Speak not your tongue.
Speak only this way.
Think only this way."
Throwing blindfolds over our eyes.

But, lache pas la patate.
Freedom is for everyone.
It comes in many, many, forms.
The chevrette can be cooked many ways.
Don't let the cocodril, the beast, keep you at bay.

This is a large land.
We are all entitled to the joie de vivre.

Our ancestors fought for us to be free.
Not to be a pauve ti bete hiding in some tree.
Ha, the demon would love for you to scream.
"Jabandonne!"
But dare you not.
Our way is not to hide.
Our way is to speak, not hide.

It's what America is all about.
No doubt, instead stand tall and shout.
Shout with all your might.
With all your might never give up the fight.
For after night comes the dawn.
And after dawn the daylight.
And in the daylight we can all fais do-do.
We can all have a boucherie.
We can all play a hand of bourre.
We can all stand tall.
And never fall, never fall.

Humanity Begins

From essential clay we came.
All humanity the same.

Freedom's Needs

Freedom whispers softly in the soft wind.
Unsuspecting of one demising sin.
Unable to speak for itself or any other.
A concept derived in minds of people.
Sometimes caught, trashed, trampled by politics.
In the name of what is right or so wrong.
Without a thought about consequences.
With it we travel far, wide, with calm eyes.
Without it we live in constant, cold, fear.
Constantly looking to see who is near.
A need to be groomed, fertilized, secured.
Growth impossible without constant care.
Here today, gone tomorrow, a real threat.
Protecting it so our heritage lives.

Mind Body Spirit

As we age some things happens to us all.
Nothing stops the eventuality.
Nothing stops the human march to the fall.
Some find a way to ease finality.
Our bodies age and fall apart in time.
The spirit inside helps us be sublime.
A strength inside, secure, waiting its chance.
Waiting to help cure vernal flu dances.
Be not afraid to seek soul redemption.
Each body needs internal salvation.
Limiting yourself to the outside world.
A waste to be spiritually curled.
The spirit helps the body strongly heal.
Helping us survive this human ordeal.

Wings of Life

Ten thousand wings silent, waiting.
A glint of sacred sunlight, the light of life,
Peeks it rays across quiet skies.
A slow deep, primordial, rumble begins.
Sounds of life, honking, calling.
Wings of flight, first a few.
Then an explosion…wings with desire.
Flapping to life, catching the wind.
Hurtling skyward, another day.
Wings of migration, wings of life.
From young to old, making the passage.
Passed down for centuries, millennia, eons.
Passageways coded into their minute DNA.
Ten thousand wings, again, for the millionth time, finding their way.
Existing, mating, eating, surviving another day.

Changes

Poets used to take time writing a poem.

Words written on unlined parchment paper.

Then scratched out, rewritten many, many, many times.

Using quill pens, wells of ink, they daily wrote.

Often for the rich, who could pay the price.

To put food on the table for families.

Before paper came much oral poetry.

Homer, a wandering bard with epic tales.

The Iliad grooming poetic history.

Now we write on paper of slick, pure glass.

No pen, no paper, no ink, just digits.

Words found, stored, electronic spirits.

Nonetheless needing to be prodigious.

The poets quest remains a sole widget.

Tomorrow Shall Arrive

Tomorrow I will awake, shower and shave.
Eat breakfast and go to work.
I won't have to be exceedingly brave.
I won't have to walk with the smirk.

I'll do my job.
Earn my bread.
Then go home with the rest..
Watch the news and shake my head.

Wondering how anyone on the left.
Or anyone on the right.
Can say they represent me.
Then go to the bathroom and take a pee.

Eat a good super with a beer or two
Sit with my iPad and pen a poem.
Or some lines without content or emotional glue.
Hoping that the words, no matter how obtuse, keep flowing.

I can do all that and more without being sore.
But if they stop me from riding my bike.
Or if they say I can't walk next to the seashore.
Or if they get riled up when told to take a hike.
Well, well, that will be close to the end.
When I can't call Trump, Biden, or Pelosi cads.
Well, that's when the stick doesn't bend.
That's when we all get the "sads."
When we are told exactly what cannot be said.

When they hand down instructions on how to make our beds.
When they dictate what words can go into our poems.
That is when we will realize that freedom is dead.

Have we come dangerously close?
Is freedom soon to be ghost?
Shelby dressed in Mao Zedong clothes?
What do you love the most?

Sitting by the Road

I sit here on the edge of the road.
Wondering if I can carry this heavy load.
I wanted freedom.
And you gave it to me.
Now I can see.

I've wandered down so many streets and avenues.
My mind has turned so often at every bend.
Now I just want some time, so I can send
These words, this heartfelt plea.
Then maybe you will understand what it means to be free.

Can you hear me?
Are you still there for me to see?
Is there still hope between us?
After all my wanderings.
After all my loneliness.

Some days are less confusing.
Others, I know I have made a terrible mess.
What I would give to be confused less.
I no longer find myself so amusing
I must confess.

Sitting alone on the edge of a road.
Wishing I was home with you.
If your sweet, tender, arms.
Away from all these worldly harms.
I can only dream, I guess.

Standing at the edge of the road.
Head tucked down against the rain and wind.
A first step, with my soul deeply skinned.
On my way home now.
On my way home now.

A Somber Life

A somber life is my long narrow path.
One filled with joy, sorrow, and some strong wrath.
Wondering about many hidden truths.
Truths that need no worldly, human made proofs.
I wander down streets made of gold, silver, bronze.
Amongst ancient gods full of healthy brawn.
Striking blows, strong, hard, swift, with molten axe.
Bowing only to those who vanquish them.
Standing tall amongst all mankind, condemn.
Those gods of ancient times long gone, elapsed.
My path, no longer following old ways
Sees new light, strong light, sure light always here.
Often fleeting, a shadow, but sometimes very near.
A light that no person need dread or fear.

You Have to See

The door opened, then slammed.
She knew it was coming.
It was after seven.
Alcohol vapors wafted from his breath.
From his clothes.
From his very essence.

"Bitch, where's my food!" he screamed.
Storming into the kitchen.
Almost falling.
God, she wished he had.
This was not good, this was bad.
As he slumped into the nearest chair.

Three sets of small eyes.
Hiding as best they could.
Watching every movement.
Wondering if it would be a belt night.
Hoping it wasn't so.
Knowing it probably would be.

Maybe this time…
Maybe she would…
Maybe they all could.
But maybe he would just eat.
Then fall asleep.
In his own vomit.
Quick, leave while he is eating.
Be quiet like church mice!

No TV, no music, no noise.
Daddy was home…the monster was here.
Daddy, please leave us alone.
Mommy, keep him away…we pray.

Maybe we can sleep next door again.
The Smiths knew about…
But no one would ever tell.
Daddy was a well-known man.
A fixture in our town.
A man of great respect.

But, behind closed doors…
Behind curtains drawn.
While the lights were low.
When no one could see.
We got to see the real he.
Firsthand not from any grandstand.

Mommy didn't work.
Daddy liked it so.
Stay home, keep the house clean!
Have my food ready and shut up!
A prisoner in her own home.
The cruelest guard to ever wear a wedding ring.

Not any house you know?
Purely some fantasy rantings?
Guess again.
Look around.
Open your eyes.
That beast might very well live next door.

Individuality

On the day you are born.
You are your own.
Unique in every way.
As you grow,
Experiences keep shaping your mold,
Even as you find someone to hold.
With love, individuality becomes even grander.
Security, freedom, warmth,
The waters that let you grow.
No person is an Island.
We swim the same currents with others.
But, ah, how we swim, the strokes we make.
Those help determine our path,
Our fate.
Even those that bend low
Can be strong.
The winds may be mighty.
They might alter our growth.
But our branches still produce leaves.
Our roots still strongly anchor us.
And our branches still provide homes
To many others.
Individuality with constant compassion.
Uniqueness with solemn understanding
Acceptance with an eye to the future.
Found in each new tree.
To be nurtured in you, them, us, and me.

CPSIA information can be obtained
at www.ICGtesting.com
Printed in the USA
LVHW052226140723
752120LV00005B/80